LICK EM ON – I'M OFF

DAVID A PROSSER

Best Wishes

Pen Press

First published in Great Britain

All paper used in the printing of this book has been made from wood grown in managed, sustainable forests.

ISBN13: 978-1-78003-238-2

Printed and bound in the UK
Pen Press is an imprint of
Indepenpress Publishing Limited
25 Eastern Place
Brighton
BN2 1GJ

A catalogue record of this book is available from the British Library

Cover design by Jacqueline Abromeit

With kind permission from Carl Chinn
the photographs on pages 35, 49, 78 and 79
are from the Birmingham Lives
The Carl Chinn Archive

With kind permission of Birmingham Library Services
photograph on page 26 Bulls Head Pub
the photographs on the front cover
top
showing the entrance of the Wolseley Works
Drews Lane, Washwood Heath
bottom
Stewarts and Lloyds works entrance in
Wheelwright Road off Bromford Lane
Birmingham

The photograph opposite (David with Irene) was taken outside my then girlfriend's house, 132 Timberley Lane, Shardend Birmingham 34. We were both at the tender age of sixteen and very much in love. We had only known each other for fourteen days; it was the Sunday 27th of March 1960 when the photograph was taken.

She was so pretty I could not believe I would ever be so blessed.

That time in my life was certainly heaven sent.

My grateful thanks to the artist

Graham Wilson

For all the line drawings and art work

That are in this book

EMPLOYMENT CARDS – KNOWN AS INSURANCE CARDS

When one became fifteen and left school in 1958, you were given the address of the insurance office near the Birmingham city centre. There you were given what they called insurance cards. Those cards had to be handed in to the employer of the firm you were going to work for – factory, office, shop or building firm. Every week that you worked there the office person put a stamp on the cards. When you handed in your notice and were leaving that employer, you had to make sure they had put the correct amount of stamps on the cards; it was not uncommon for an office person to miss putting on the last weeks stamp. If at the end of the year you were short of stamps on your card, the National Assistance Boards (now known as Social Security) made you pay for the missing stamps. When a boss upset me I would say, "Lick 'em on, I'm off", meaning lick my stamp for that week onto my card, I'm leaving your employment.

I wrote this book for my three children, Anthony, Wendy and Matthew, whom I love deeply.

I dedicate this book to my ex wife Irene who saw this book through with me to fruition.

MY WIFE

Before you read this book I feel I must make it known that my ex wife, Irene, encouraged me to do whatever I said I couldn't do. She sat down with me when I felt low and thought I would never be any good and amount to anything, and she taught me more than any of the teachers that had me for ten years. She put up with my illiteracy, stupidity, my ignorance and the poverty we endured because of me. She suffered with me and our children and never complained – she always said, "So long as I am with you, I would live in a shed in the middle of nowhere." She poured faith, happiness and love into my children and me; she is the backbone of my family. Irene, my devoted ex wife who never ever gave up on me, I owe her for what I am and have now. She was my tower of strength, my back bone. "Dave," she told me, "I love you so much I would give up my life for you," which brought tears to my eyes. She still says that to this very day – even though we are divorced.

CONTENTS

Photos and Illustrations

INTRODUCTION

I met my wife, Irene Yvonne Parker, of 132 Timberley Lane, Shard End, on Sunday 13th March 1960 at the Castle Cinema, which was situated in the Castle Bromwich area of Birmingham – I was 16 years of age. We married on 23rd December 1961 at All Saints Church, Shard End. We had three children, Anthony, Wendy and Matthew. My dad was William John Prosser, my mom was Dora Louisa Prosser (nee King) and they lived at 38 Plowden Road, Glebe Farm, Stechford, in the Birmingham area – that is where I was born.

STARTING IN THE WORLD OF WORKING ADULTS

I was born in 1943, on the 30th October; we were still at war with Germany, and they were bombing and devastating our wonderful country – I was growing up in hardship and poverty.

When it came to my time in December 1958 to leave school, jobs were plentiful as England was still being rebuilt. I could walk out of one job, walk across the road and get another, which I did many times through my years of my working life. Then came the depression in the 1980's when one had to think twice about leaving one's employment. We all thought it wouldn't happen again, and here we are in the 21st century – another depression.

VARIETY IS THE SPICE OF LIFE

I worked on the Chelmsley Wood Estate, for the building firm known as Bryant's, driving a dumper truck taking compo to the bricklayers, who were building a blue brick wall; it has since been rendered in pebble dash, it's in a road known as Moorend Avenue. I only stayed at that job for six weeks, now there's a surprise. I worked casual for lots of different firms – I drove a lorry for an Irish man for a month, when the motorway M42 was being constructed in the Castle Bromwich area.

I worked casual for a firm cleaning rust off machines that was caused by flood damage earlier that year; I worked in the main fortnight's holiday, the last week in July and the first week in August, most big factories closed down in those two weeks, so they set to getting all the necessary cleaning and repairs done. I worked all over the country working casual inside factories in those main two holiday weeks. Yes I would do any job for a short time; I most certainly had the variety and the spice of life.

I worked on farms all over the country. I did nearly all the jobs a farmer would do: vegetable farming, cattle farming, even milking, and I worked on the railway delivering to farms all around Warwickshire, Staffordshire and Leicestershire. In those days those farms were isolated, quiet and tranquil; it was a real pleasure in the summer, not quite so good in the winter. I did sink down to the axle on one occasion, which cost the railways, and I got a good telling off for that – I never did it again.

I even joined the army when I was twenty-nine; I did seven years in the pioneers, I went all over the continent driving, and a few years later I joined the H. S. F. Home Service Forces, commonly known as Dad's Army. I did seven years training, so for the defence of England I trained for fourteen years and I loved every minute of it I would love to be part of it today but they don't like slow old men in the armed forces.

MY FIRST JOB

I left school in December 1958, at the tender age of fifteen. I'm a working man now I've left school, I thought to myself. Man indeed; I wasn't even an old 15, still very much a child. Life has a habit of taking away the boy, and then hits one with what we call manhood. How did I find out I was still a boy? When I went for a job at the Metropolitan Camel Carriage Works I was asked to sign my signature. I was horrified, I never knew what the difference was between a signature and initials; what do I do now? I was terrified, so I put my initials; the foreman looked and said, "No son, your signature." I knew then at that moment what the difference was. I've never forgotten that moment; I was so frightened my throat was dry, my speech had gone and I was shaking – I needed the toilet and fast.

I realised at that moment in time I was virtually unemployable; I couldn't read or write very well, I could just about write my name – maths were non-starters. I was fifteen and nearly totally illiterate. Well I never got that job; I did some time later. I walked homeward feeling very much the failure I was, I headed for the park as I did so many times before with my friends as a school boy. I was alone and very low in my self esteem, asking myself what am I to do? What can I do? I'm nothing, I know nothing. Adults could not see or understand a boy screaming inside himself, please someone help me. No one could, that was down to me, so life had just started for me. I must work out how to get started, I was telling myself. I sat on that bank by the river for nearly half a day, my head was all over the place; I got up and headed homewards.

My mom was always kind to me. "Hello, son," she said as I walked into the kitchen via our back door, "did you get a job?"

"I filled in an ap... ap..."

"You mean an application form, son."

"Yes, Mom, that's it."

"Well, keep trying," she replied.

I was drained of energy so I went and I sat on my bed, to be honest I was close to tears, I was lost in a world of adults. I sat on my bed just as

I did on the river bank, clueless, I had no brains. Some of my friends' parents took their children to have interviews, but I never wanted my parents to take me around to all the factories, I just needed some advice and guidance. I was screaming inside myself please someone help me, why oh why won't someone help me? I was keyed up, so exhausted from all the torment that I fell asleep.

Mom woke me from my sleep asking if I was all right as I looked very pale. "I'm OK, Mom," I told her.

I could not face my friends that evening, so I went to bed at 7pm only to be shaken the next morning by my dad. "Come on, son," said Dad, "you have got to find a job today." It was 6.45a.m. "Early start, son, beat the others to it. Welcome to the working classes." Thanks Dad, I thought.

Getting up early in the mornings was not one of the things in life I liked doing. With no money to my name and no food in my belly, well a piece of toast, I started to walk the streets to find employment. It was a cold day, no underwear, no overcoat and still I had pumps with holes in, (that's living, eh?) the crutch of my trousers was ripped; more air vents in my clothes than there was material, even my coat was too small for me, so I couldn't fasten it up, it was one my mom got for me from a jumble sale just before I left school – it cost the sum of 4d four pence.

Any road up, I kept walking and found myself almost in town, (Birmingham city that is) when I saw a factory that restored and, I think, made guns. I walked into the reception area, it was dark looking, not very well lit, very quiet, even a little bit creepy, with dark oak panels and a smell I had never smelt before. There was a beautiful counter, very long and very wide and very dark in colour, and glass cases on every wall displaying guns, bullets, tools and all sorts of wonderful looking items. I was captivated; it was so silent I could hear myself breathing. Silently staring at all those wonderful cases, when the silence was broken by a very soft and feminine voice saying, "Can I help you?" She said with a smile, "You should have rung the bell."

"Erm... erm..." What do I say? I was asking myself. My nerves were shot once again; no one had ever told me how to approach an employer.

"Well, young man, how can I help you?" she asked again.

I blurted out, "Got any jobs?" Well a shocked look appeared on her very pretty face.

"I beg your pardon, that's no way to find employment."

I said sorry with a bowed head and her face changed to a soft smile again as instantly she saw a little boy that was worried to death and didn't know what he was doing. "You sit there," she told me, pointing to an old leather chair – I could have been back in the Dickensian era. A couple of minutes passed when a very large man appeared, his face was round, red in colour with little round wire framed glasses on the end of his nose. With a deep but posh voice he asked, "So you are looking for employment are you?"

"Yes sir," I replied.

"Where have you worked before, what experience have you?"

"I've just left school," I replied, very nervously.

"Oh, I see," he said with doubt in his voice. "All right, can you start in the morning?"

"Yes sir," I replied with a surprised tone to my voice.

"We will show you what the job is all about and how we work tomorrow. Your wages will start at two pounds ten shillings a week."

"Thank you, sir," I replied.

"We start at 7.45am sharp; I will see you tomorrow," the man told me.

The lady I saw when I first entered the building gave me a beautiful smile. "See you tomorrow," she said.

"Thank you lady." I was feeling very good at that moment in time. I've got a job, I'm a working man – I was full of the joys of spring. My mom will be pleased, I thought, as I walked up the road to head for home. I kept saying to myself, I've got a job, I've got a job! I couldn't remember what the name of that firm was, but I did remember it was in Loveday Street.

As I reached the main road where the buses ran, I saw an old school mate of mine with his mom, waiting at the bus stop, "Hiya," I shouted, "where have you been?"

"My mom took me to the co-op bakery employment department for a job delivering bread. I did an I.Q. test but I failed it," he told me.

"Where have you been?" asked his mother.

With my chest out I replied, “I’ve just got a job at a gunsmith’s.”

“What that gunsmith’s in Loveday Street, over there?” she said, pointing to the road.

“Yes,” I replied.

“Well I would not let him work in an old fashioned place like that,” she said, pointing to her son. “I would not allow him to mess about with guns. They would take anybody there, that’s why you got the job,” she said to me. I felt so deflated, even hurt, all my excitement vanished with the blink of an eye. She was upset because her son failed to get his job. I was really hurting at that moment, and then she asked me, “Where are you going now, David?”

“Home,” I replied.

“Oh I see, so you will be getting on the bus with us then.”

“No,” I replied, “I haven’t any money.”

“It’s a long walk, David, it will take you ages; it must be seven to ten miles.”

Just as she said that, a bus pulled up. She smiled as she got on the bus and said, “Bye, David, enjoy your walk.”

“Bye,” I shouted as the bus pulled away. I wonder why she wouldn’t lend me the three pence, I thought. As she sat down and looked out of the window she gave a big smile and waved. It did take me ages to get home, how long I’m not sure.

As I walked through the back door into the kitchen, Mom asked how I had got on. I very proudly said, “I start work tomorrow.” She was so pleased it made me feel good. I ate my tea very quickly; mind you I usually did anyway.

I went to see my mate Trevor to tell him the good news. He thought it was great and congratulated me. “I’m very happy for you Dave.” I felt quite relaxed at that moment, being with my mate who I had grown up with and had done so much with as a child.

Next morning up very early, I tucked my collar into my shirt to wash my neck as I had done all my young days, then I dried myself on a wet towel as usual as we still only had one, and using the family comb that we all used that was always on the windowsill next to the sink in the kitchen, I combed my hair.

There was Kathleen, Doreen, Janet, me, John, Mom, Dad and Doreen's husband, and we all washed in the kitchen, dried ourselves on the same towel, and used the same comb. The kitchen sink was the only sink in the house in those times. A sink wasn't fitted in the bathroom when the house was built but one was fitted at a later date. The comb was a blue nylon one and it was used for many, many years – no money was wasted in our house, I can tell you. So I ate my one piece of toast, drank my cup of tea and put my two pieces of bread and butter in my pocket, which was my lunch for dinnertime. Dad had the meat on his sandwiches; well the men were always given the most as they were the bread winners as the saying goes. Mom gave me sixpence for my bus fare, three pence there and three pence back – that was a child's fare. I walked from the bus to the factory, which was only a few strides from the bus stop. I walked into the factory through the entrance, the men's entrance, the other entrance was marked 'Girls Entrance' above the door, I think carved in sand stone. I was shaking with nerves as I walked in.

I was greeted by a little man wearing a cow gown that looked bigger than him, it looked like his head was trying to hide inside it, and it almost touched the floor – it looked really funny on him. "Have you brought your cards with you?" he asked, looking me up and down as he spoke. I gave him my cards. "Follow me," he said in a frightening voice. He showed me to a bench where there was what seemed like a pile of rifles. "I will show you how to strip these rifles, so pay attention." By this time I was terrified. "When you have stripped one with this sanding block," he was showing me, "I want you to sand the butt of the rifle till all the varnish has gone." Still he looked me up and down, muttering something.

"Sorry," I said, "I didn't hear what you just said."

"It doesn't matter now, get on with your work, I want a good job doing of those butts."

It took me ages to do the first one; my arm was really aching so I stopped to rest it. The little man came from nowhere. "Come on you lazy idiot, you will have to buck your ideas up. I don't think you will be any good here."

I had only been there two hours; he growled at me, every time he said anything to me. When I came to strip another rifle I had forgotten how to do it and now I was really panicking, I was afraid to ask. In the end I had to. "I've shown you once," he snarled, "you must pay attention." So I did four butts.

"Where is the toilet?" I asked a boy who I think was a teenager, and off I went. When I came back the little man was waiting for me, his face was like thunder.

"Where have you been to?"

"The toilet," I replied.

"Already? Well don't let me catch you going again till this evening." He was really growling at me, his face was all screwed up with anger. I will show him, I thought. I will work really hard and get all these rifles done before dinner. I must have been standing funny, my legs were really aching, so I sat on the bench still doing my work, when a very loud voice from the back of me screamed "Do you want a cushion?" as I was being dragged off the bench. "Don't you ever sit on the bench!"(I'm not sure, but I don't think he liked me very much!). Well it was dinnertime and I was ready for it. "I asked, "Where do I get a cup of tea from?"

"You have to bring your own," I was told, so I ate my two bread and butter sandwiches, had a drink from the tap in the toilet and off I went outside to have a cigarette to calm my nerves. I sat on the wall; it was cold so I went back in to the factory, only to find no one was talking to me. I was finding things a little stressful by this time. Back to work, just as I reached my bench the little man came to me again snarling at me. "Did I see you smoking?"

"Yes, I smoke; my dad gave me three cigarettes this morning," I told him.

"How dare you smoke around me! You are not old enough to smoke; don't let me catch you smoking again." It was worse than being at school.

After about ten minutes he came to me and told me to go to the office and get a box, they were expecting me. The box contained sticks about two feet long, half inch thick and pointed at one end. I was shown downstairs where there were many machines. It was a very big room there must have been twenty or so machines down there, no one worked on them, they were there and used only when needed, so I was shown how to put the sticks in the machine which was a lathe. With emery cloth I was told to sand them. This is easy, I thought, I will work hard then the little man will be pleased with me. When I had done what was in the box, I took them back to the office and got another box off them – what they were for I have no idea. I did five boxes altogether. The lady in the office said, "Well done, you have worked hard." That was very pleasing to hear, it made me feel good. "Have you enjoyed your first day?" she asked.

"Yes," I said; I was lying, I didn't really, that little man made me nervous and worried me; I was a bag of nerves when he was around.

First day done, I ran out of that factory as fast as I could and got on my bus. I went upstairs, you could smoke upstairs on buses in those days, I got my cigarette out but before I lit it I looked around to see if the little man was watching, he had got me in a state. I was glad to get home that evening.

The next morning I arrived on time. I was saying good morning but no one spoke to me. I went up to the teenager and said, "That job I had yesterday, I liked it, do you do them all the time?"

"We don't have those very often, all the ones you did weren't good enough, I worked over last night and did them all again."

I felt terrible and I thought I had done a good job, why didn't they show me what I was doing wrong, I was thinking.

The little man came up to me and said, "Carry on doing those butts you did yesterday."

Well, I thought, he seems better today; I will do a good job, he might start to be nice to me. So I started sanding the butts. It was almost dinner time and the little man had not been near me so I started to feel relaxed. This is not so bad today, I thought. It was about half an hour to dinner time when a lad came up to me very smartly dressed, he even wore a tie, I had never owned a tie. "Have you just started?" I asked him.

"Yes," he said to me. "How long have you worked here?"

"I only started yesterday," I replied. He then went to talk to the other people that worked there.

Dinner time came; I ate my two pieces of toast, and went to the toilet for a drink of water. As I came out I noticed the new boy having a cup of tea. I looked at him dressed in clothes that would have been my Sunday best, that's a laugh I never had Sunday best since the day I was born! Next to that boy I looked like a tramp.

After lunch the little man was talking to the new boy really nice, why didn't he talk to me nicely like he is talking to the new boy? He came to my bench and said, "Stand away a minute, I'm going to show this lad how to do this job." He even gave him an apron – he never ever mentioned an apron to me. "Ok son, you carry on with those," he said to him.

I wonder what he is going to ask me to do now, I was thinking. "Right," he said as he turned towards me, "the boss wants a word with you in the main office."

As I knocked on the door I was a little nervous. He called me in, it was more like being in the Dickensian era than the office area, it was dark oak panelling floor to ceiling, with old portraits all-around the walls and very old looking leather chairs. As I was looking at the portraits I almost forgot where I was. "They are my ancestors," he said. "Look son, I have bad news for you. I've taken on too many staff, I put all the names in a hat and yours came out." And I believed him. He handed me my cards and said, "I have paid you a little more than you have earned, one pound seven shillings." He handed me the money in cash in my hand, no wage packet, he then said, "Don't go back into the factory; I want you to leave the premises straight away." One and a half days and I was sacked, fired, kicked out, given the boot. I was still wet behind the ears, had seen nothing, done nothing, been nowhere in life and I wasn't given a chance. Welcome to the world of working life, I said to myself, that little man saw how poor I looked and took a dislike to me, well maybe I was a bad worker and I didn't know it, all I can say is that I hope any offspring of that little man receive better treatment than he dished out to me.

I have taken on too many staff – your name came out of the hat, don't go back into the work shop, leave the premises now.

CLARKS

My sister Janet worked at Clarks, in the Nechells area of Birmingham, St Clements Road I think it was in, a couple of hundred yards from the Saltley gasworks. They produced all sorts of cables for motor bikes, cars, push bikes and many others. I went there for a job after I had the sack from the gunsmiths. I had an interview and was asked how I had heard about this factory, and how did I know there was a vacancy going there. “My sister works here,” I explained, and told them who she was and where she worked in the factory.

“She is a good worker; I hope you are as good. Ok you can start tomorrow and bring your cards with you,” I was told. My mom was very pleased.

Next morning, same old routine, tucked my shirt collar in to wash my face and neck, dried myself on the wet towel and used the old nylon blue comb after getting all the hair out of it. Mom had made me egg sandwiches – well I had taken some money home from the gunsmith’s!

What a wonderful atmosphere! Everyone was kind, I was even given a cigarette; I loved it. When dinnertime came the foreman came to me. “Have you any tea, Dave?”

“No,” I replied.

“Come with me; you can share with us till you sort out with the others – they put a shilling a week into a kitty, and that pays for the tea, milk and sugar. Have you brought any sandwiches with you?”

“Yes, thank you,” I said to him.

“Good,” he replied, “I would have bought you one from the café; you could have paid me back out of your first week’s wages.” What a difference from the gunsmith’s, I was happy, so I got a cup from home and had tea at work. So all firms ain’t like that gunsmith’s and like that little man that was buried inside his cow gown, I thought to myself, this firm was friendly.

I was shown in detail how to do all the different jobs. When I was putting the ferrules on the end of the cables, I didn’t do them quite right, I was worried to death and afraid to ask the foreman to show me again, but I had to. When I went to him, he said, "You look worried sick, whatever is the matter?"

I explained to him my problem. With his hand on my shoulder he said, "It's all right, Dave, don't worry, you will soon get the hang of it."

I was so relieved. There was a wonderful family atmosphere every day in that factory; it was a pleasure to go to work. There were a few people that worked there from where I lived in Glebe Farm, Stechford. My next door neighbour Beryl worked there. Everything was going good, £3-10-0 a week and not a soul screaming or growling at me. I was given a job soldering the ends of the cables, putting what they called barrels on the end of them, then with a bunch of them I very slowly put the ends of the cables with the barrels on the end of them into a big bowl of melted hot solder, this operation welded the barrels firmly to the cable – it was a very satisfying job. After that I was asked to put the cables into the outer cases, those were for motor bikes. It was a little tricky at first but I got quite fast at it.

My sister Janet worked alongside a girl that lived just around the corner from the factory; she was so pretty, I just couldn't stop staring at her. My sister used to go to her house for lunch, and I went with her on a few occasions. As I sat looking at her with all the desires of youth, I was thinking I wish you would go out with me; of course it never happened. The first time I walked into her house I was shocked, it was a little back to back house. I lived in poverty and knew hard times, but that house looked like it needed knocking down – her upbringing was even lower than mine. She was always well dressed and very polite; I on the other hand suited that house very well, course and common. Any road up, I worked at Clarks for four months. I was getting bored by this time, I had learned how to do all the jobs, I wanted a new challenge, and so I handed in my notice. The foreman asked me to reconsider as he liked the way I worked, he said, "You are a good worker it's a shame to lose you."

I said, "No, I'm leaving."

"Well, if you ever want to come back, I will give you your job back," the foreman told me. So I left. I have fond memories of that firm; the kindness, the friendliness and the family atmosphere. Yes, time to move on to pastures new, I thought.

An elderly gentleman once said to me, "Son, variety is the spice of life; do as many different things in life as you can." Yes, I have certainly done that, as you will see as you go through my life with me in this book.

METROPOLITAN CARRIAGE WORKS

The second time I tried to get a job at the carriage works, I got a job working in the rivet shop. The day I started I was very happy, as I loved the railways; it felt really good to be part of them. I was a very tiny cog in a massive machine – well a tooth on a cog would be more like it. It was based in the Saltley area of Birmingham, and my dad worked there for many years; he worked there through the war years.

He was a radial driller, and he did his share of fire watching, well most of the time, he sometimes paid a man to do his fire watching. If he did that, he went into the tote, that was a club on the Alum Rock Road, just up the road from his firm. He told my mom he had been fire watching – typical male. He told me his wages were £25 a week, and all he gave my mom was £4 to keep six children at that time. I never knew how he made that sort of money in those days, but my uncle Bob was the manager there, maybe that had something to do with it.

As I walked through the different shops, as the different departments were called, I was staggered at the size of the place and the amount of people that worked there. I was taken to the foreman who showed me my job. There was a frame of what looked like a box with two thick cables going to it, and a foot pedal. When this was pushed down with the foot it opened a jaw with a pair of tongs. A rivet was picked out of a sack, there were a few sacks of different size rivets for use on different jobs, and the rivet was placed between the jaws when the foot was taken off the pedal. The rivet started to heat up – it went cherry red to white hot, that was the moment it had to be taken out or it melted, so with rivet in the tongs I had to throw it to wherever the men were working; sometimes I threw it a few yards, sometimes only a couple of feet. The machine was at the end of the gangways, not many people walked down those gangways, when the rivets were being thrown. The rivets had to be used before they went red, but many a time they were not hot enough, as they tried to ball the ends over – boy did they swear when that happened, and getting them back out could sometimes be a problem. They even had a man check them and if he found one or two were not tight enough he would tell them to replace them, and the bad language started again. When I threw them, sometimes one would bounce over his boot, boy did that annoy them, they used to threaten to do all sorts to me; of course I played the innocence, I would say, "sorry mate, was that too hard? I'm trying to get the distance right." By that time the rivet wasn't hot enough. What annoyed them was they got paid for the amount of work they did.

After a couple of months they were short of manpower in the saw mill. I was transferred to the mill, and I was very happy in there, I love the smell of wood. That mill was the most laid back workshop I have ever worked in. The most work I ever did was about two hours a day; I swept and cleaned the machine just for something to do. My job there was to stand at the back of the machine and take whatever was cut and stack it on a trolley; I was forever picking up the off cuts of timber and smelling it, I loved the aroma. I think it was pitch pine, I'm not certain, it was pine anyway.

We only cut timber for carriages. In the compound out the back of the saw mill were thousands of pounds worth of timber being seasoned in the fullness of time, some piles were dated war time, what I didn't know was any newcomer to the saw mill was chased round and round the timber piles till one was really sweaty, then they threw you into the sawdust pit under the machine – that was very uncomfortable I can tell you, as you calmed down and stopped sweating, you had to strip off, or itch all afternoon. Machinists mate, that was what I was, and had to make the tea for the machinists mornings, dinnertime and afternoon. Each of the lads had so many men to look after; I had nine Billy cans, nine machinists to look after, I got to know every little thing about each man and just how they liked their tea. I used to put the tea and sugar in each can; carrying nine Billy cans full of hot tea was a little tricky at times when walking back trying not to spill them. The cans were not marked, but I got to know each one like it was my own. It was about thirty or forty yards to walk from where the boiling urn was. One dinnertime an office girl was running fast down the gangway, and she ran into me and knocked all the cans out of my hands; she never stopped to pick them up, she just shouted sorry and carried on. At that time I had only been doing the cans a couple of weeks so I guessed what tea and sugar they had in them. Of course I got it all wrong; boy did they moan! Afternoon tea was ok though, when the cans got too stained with the tea all the lads used ashes to clean them. One of my men asked, “How do you get the can so clean?”

I told him, “With ash.”

He had a fit. “Don’t do mine anymore like that.” That news went around the shop floor like fire, all the men told their tea boys not to clean them that way, and we said we wouldn’t any more – of course we did, but they never knew. Me and my big mouth!

We got a shilling a week off each of our men we made tea for, that 9 shillings came in very handy at the end of the week. When the shift was over, every boy in that mill had to clean down the machine and use the air lines to blow the sawdust down the pit; sometimes it was easier with a broom. Some dinnertimes I went and sat with my dad in the machine shop – it wasn’t ever so clean. Dad did the drilling of the axle boxes and the wagon chasses. He had six machines on the go because the chasses were very long so six holes at a time made the job easier. One dinnertime I knocked dad’s Billy can over, he wasn’t very happy; I never sat with him again after that.

I liked the smell of suds; it’s a milky looking liquid that runs over the drills as they are cutting through the metal, it kept them from getting hot.

As I mentioned before, uncle Bob was a manager there; he never once came to say hello, in fact I only saw him twice that I remember all through my life. I remember those two times because he bought me an ice cream, 6d they were, we only got 3d ones usually and that was on very rare occasions, mind you it made it a special treat.

After three months I was starting to get bored again, yes bored, so I handed in my notice. Is it boredom or am I lazy? I’m not sure, well new adventure here I come, I used to say to myself. It’s strange you know, all the places I worked at I used to look around to try and remember what certain walls looked like and the washrooms and the inside of certain rooms, and think I won’t be seeing any of this again after today, and for a reason I can’t explain I felt sad. I’ve had that many jobs I can't remember most of them, but I can a few.

As I left this firm it was the start of the industrial holidays, this was when the factories closed down and the industrial cleaners and maintenance workers went into the factories to clean or do any repairs that needed to be done. I was glad I had left because this was when my friends asked me to go with them to Upton on Severn camping.

UPTON-ON-SEVERN

Seven months after leaving school in the July of 1959, two of my friends, Maurice and Johnny asked me if I wanted to go to Upton on Severn camping, only for a week. It was in the main two weeks holiday when all the factories closed down – the last week in July and the first week in August, that was how it was then. The camp site was right on the river's edge, and we could go swimming every day, which we all loved, so I agreed to go. That was on the Friday evening, and we all went the next morning.

None of us had much money; we did what we had always done, did everything with nothing, well almost. That evening Trevor and me went to the Beaufort Cinema along with my younger brother John, but unknown to us he had a water pistol with him. Trevor started to chat up two girls that that were sitting in front of us when they suddenly jumped up with a sort of a quiet scream – my brother John was squirting his water pistol under the seat onto their legs and they couldn't understand what was going on. John sat up and made believe he knew nothing about it, well not until they caught him doing it that is. Well we went on the bus with them to take them home; John got off and went home, Trevor and me stayed with the girls on the bus, and we all got off at the Mackadown, Tile Cross. The two girls lived about twenty yards from the bus stop; we talked for about three quarters of an hour I suppose it was. "Can I see you again?" I asked one of them.

"Yes please, I would like that, tomorrow," she replied.

"Oh I can't," I told her, "I've agreed to go camping with my mates, to Upton on Severn for the week."

"Don't go," she said with a sad look on her face, "I want to see you tomorrow."

I was so tempted; I really wanted to see her again. "I will meet you here tomorrow night, at seven o'clock," I told her.

"Yes," she said, "I would like that." So we said goodnight – I never even attempted to kiss her, (I never did have any brains or guts) and we parted. I'm not sure if Trevor turned up the following evening, I've never asked him, thinking about it, so me and Trevor walked home . I never did see that girl again; I can't even remember what she looked like or even her name.

Yes I went camping to Upton on Severn near Worcester, as I said none of us had enough money for a week's holiday, not even enough to feed ourselves let alone pay for anything extra. We took a primus stove, a loaf, some tinned beans, butter and two tins of soup, that was it. Three growing hungry lads were about to experience weight loss without wanting to. We cycled to Upton on Severn, pitched our tent, and had bread and butter and a plate of beans on a lovely sunny afternoon. Moored on the river where we were was a boat that had been dragged off the bottom of the riverbed, it was in a right old state, so we used it for our diving board. We had great fun. When we had had enough, we dried ourselves on our hand towels, yes hand towels, we draped them over our tent to dry, which you would, that was the only place to dry them anyway.

That evening we explored the town hoping to find a couple of beauties, but no luck, any road up we had breakfast next morning, soup and bread and butter, and that was us – skint. On our site there were lots of tents and caravans, and the smell of bacon cooking was more than flesh and blood could stand, especially for young teenagers who just lived to eat. Well, as you can imagine, us three growing lads were starving. Next to the site was an orchard of egg plums, we lived on them for the whole two days, and no, we never did get stomach ache.

A very observant lady who was caravanning a few yards from our tent came over to us and asked, "Why do you boys keep eating those plums?"

"We ain't got any food or money left to buy any food," we told her. Nearly an hour later she came over to us with a tray, it must have been three foot long by eighteen inches wide, and on it were sixteen sausages and they were swimming in tinned tomatoes, not in the tins I might add, just the tomatoes, she even gave us a loaf of bread – we shared it equally. It was like a feast we had never had or so it seemed, to three starving boys. We had a few hours swim, and after that we were in top form. When night time came and we were back on the egg plums we decided to call it a day and head back home. The next morning we did just that. I love these memories; if only I had that sort of energy now! Still, it was great to be young. Happy days.

COOKS FOR CLOCKS

When I started at Cooks, the clock face makers, they were situated in the Bulls head area in Stechford. It was known as the Bulls Head because the pub was called the Bulls Head; it was a lovely building, but sadly it's now been demolished. Lots of women and young girls worked at Cooks, it was a family firm and it had a very friendly atmosphere. I worked in the degreasing room; my job was to put sheets of metal into a vat that had a liquid in the bottom of it, this was known as Trykoethylene, I think that's the right way to spell it; we always referred to it as Trike. The liquid created a mist which very slowly rose and covered the metal sheets, taking off any grease that was on them. I wore gloves as the sheets could not be touched by human flesh, as this made the metal greasy. I had a timer to set, I think it was for three minutes, when the bell rang I then waited for the Trike to evaporate. I had to very slowly take out the sheets of metal – if removed too quick it left streaky marks on the sheets, this created a problem for the ladies who before they could spin the clock circles on them, had to use a powder called Fullers Earth with a soft rag, this would rub off every streak; they got very annoyed with me when I messed up. Mind you, sometimes I did it on purpose, and used to say to them, " Well it gives you something to do," boy did that get them going – I had to move fast to avoid flying objects! After the circles were finished and the silver was put on them, they then went to a young fella to guillotine them to the sizes required.

I was in the darts team, we played every dinner time. One evening we had a darts match in the Bulls Head pub opposite the factory. Every one of our team won, all except me that is, I lost on my double. No shame; my opponent got to his double first and hit it, one of our players tried to embarrass me saying sarky things, he knew I didn't drink. "Come on, Dave, I will play you for a pint."

"Ok, let's do it," I said. We played 301, and I beat him easily.

"That was a fluke; let's play again."

"Ok, for another pint?" I asked.

"Yes, of course. I want to win my pint back," he said. Well I left him standing. I'm no good at darts; it just went right that evening.

"Another game?" I said cockily.

"No, you got lady luck on your side tonight." I gave the two pints away.

We saved every week for the Christmas party. Inside the factory a week before the party someone stole the money, the party funds. Everyone was very shocked and very hurt. The ladies took it the hardest – we all thought we were friends, yet one of us was a horrible, despicable thief. They said they knew who it was but just could not prove it. The ladies, God bless em, did what ladies always do, and they saved the day. They made cakes, trifles, sandwiches and put all the trimmings up as well; wonderful ladies, wonderful memories.

Not long after the Christmas holiday in the middle of February, I fancied a change of scenery, so I handed in my notice. I've no staying power – four and a half months it seems is about all I can manage. My longest job was at Coca Cola, most was four months. To be honest I hated going to work, but one has to earn a living.

Degreasing the metal sheets ready for the clock faces to be put on them.

The Bull's Head public house
Sadly now demolished

DOING A RUNNER

Me and my friend Johnny, who I grew up with and now worked with, always had a game of snooker every Friday after work. We were hopeless at it but we enjoyed playing – we worked at Cooks the clock face makers at that time. As we walked through the front doors of the snooker hall, along a passage, through two other doors and into the main hall, we said the same thing, we sounded like a stuck record: "Any tables free?"

He shocked us this one Friday evening by replying, "Sorry lads, I'm fully booked up, but seeing how you are regulars I will open the upstairs up for you."

It was creepy, dead quiet, with only the light on over the table. We played for an hour, and then went downstairs for a cup of tea and a packet of Cadburys short bread chocolate biscuits. When we played on the tables downstairs, it was always lights out after an hour; we would either pay for another hour or go home, but because we were upstairs on our own the light never went out. The man behind the bar switched them off by hand when we were downstairs, so we got carried away. Three and a half hours later, John said, "Dave we've been playing for three and a half hours." I was horrified; we couldn't pay for the table.

"We will have to do a runner, John," I told him. So we very quietly crept down the concrete stairs and into the street and we ran like the wind away from that hall. "We will have to stay away for a few weeks, Dave," John suggested to me, and I agreed – the boys who ran that hall were a rough bunch.

The next Friday we forgot all about doing a runner the Friday before. In we marched. "Any tables free? we were just about to ask when he got hold of us.

"I've been waiting for you pair; you owe me for three and a half hours for last Friday."

We both said together, "It wasn't us, mister, honest." I told him I hadn't been to work all that week.

“I never went out of the house till this Monday, Johnny said, “We come here all the time, we wouldn’t do that to you, you always look after us,”

“I know it was you,” he shouted.

“Honest, mister, we didn’t come in last week,” I told him.

“Right, I’m putting you on this first table next to me, you try doing a runner from here.”

We had confused him enough to put a little doubt in his mind; if he had been sure, we would have been taken round to the back of the hall and given the beatings of our lives. We were never allowed upstairs again, I felt terrible for running but it was a good beating up or risk getting away with it – we were very lucky.

After I left Cooks I got a job on the Co-op bakery as a rounds boy delivering bread. Me and Johnny didn’t meet up again for a very long time, and it was many years later before I went in to that snooker hall again.

Artist impression of the Co-op bakery in Manor Road, Stechford

ROUNDS BOY CO-OP BAKERY

It was a sunny Monday morning; I was sitting at the table eating my usual piece of toast when for a reason I can't explain, I was thinking about my first job and how much that little man disliked me for reasons I have never known. Then my thoughts went to that bus stop where I met an old school chum and his mother – not a nice memory. I thought to myself, right, I will go up town to the Birmingham city centre, and see if I can get a job at that Co-op bakery. I remembered my school chum saying he failed to get a job there.

I arrived in town via a number 14 bus. I remember the Co-op well because my mom took me there as a small boy a few times to see Father Christmas. I went to the personnel office to ask the young lady if there were any jobs going. I remembered my mistake from my first job, not to blurt out "got any jobs", so all confident, no nerves at all, I enquired, "Have you any vacancies please?"

"What are you looking for?" I was asked.

"Anything," I replied.

"We are looking for rounds boys to deliver bread in the Stechford area. Would that be too far away for you?"

I could not believe my luck! "I live in Stechford," I replied.

"You will have to take an IQ test."

Those words scared the life out of me. It was a simpleton's test, well no trouble there, I thought, there is no one simpler than me. I was shown into a room, given a sheet of paper and to my surprise it was easy; it had things like apple, orange, stone – which is the odd one out? And what is the capital of England? When I had finished I took the sheet to the reception. The young lady put a card with holes all over it on top of the sheet, looked up at me, smiled and said, "You have got the job."

I felt so good. I've passed a test! To be honest I felt a little proud, it was such an achievement for me.

I had to report to a Mr Starky at the Manor Road bakery in the Stechford area, with a note, that afternoon saying I would be starting work there the day after tomorrow. I was so excited I went to see my old school chum to tell him my good news, you know, the one I met at the bus stop with his mother. His mother said, “Oh, they are short staffed at the moment, they are taking anybody on, that is why you got the job.” Well that burst my bubble of excitement, I can tell you, but at least I got the job.

I had to go back to the main office in town the next day. There was a room full of people, and we were given a talk on the Co-op, how it started, what they did and sold and a film show on hygiene and the dos and don’ts when working for the co-op. The one thing that stuck in my mind was a man sneezing and seeing in slow motion how far the spray from his mouth travelled as he sneezed. I enjoyed that talk, funny really, I hated the word ‘classroom’, it meant learning; not being very bright, it was always traumatic for me especially when asked questions in front of a room full of people – that always scared me.

The bakery wasn’t far from my house so I hadn’t any bus fares to find, I walked there. As I walked down the hill of Manor Road towards the bakery, the smell of baking bread travelling up the hill on the wind was pure nectar to me. Every morning I would take deep lungs full of air to take in that wonderful smell.

On my arrival I was taken to the stores and given two cow gowns, this made me very happy because it covered up my bad attire – I was desperate for a new pair of shoes and trousers because the crutch of my trousers was ripped from the flies to the rear, and my pumps still had holes in. After the first day my feet were very sore as the cardboard in my pumps soon wore out. I can’t remember what my wages were for sure, £3-3/- seems to ring a few bells.

My round was all around the Stechford area. Malcolm Brown was the rounds man I worked with; he had worked for the Co-op since he was fourteen. We loaded the electric van from the deck alongside many other vans. It was a long deck, and it was loaded the same way every morning. On the right hand side on the top runners we put the uncut bread, the next two runners down were the thick and thin sliced, waxed paper wrapped bread on the floor under the trays of bread that were on wire trays. We slid two wooden trays containing the cakes and biscuits on the left and right of the van, and on the left runners we put sliced bread and the two runners below we put the cottage loaves, milk rolls, bloomers and brown Hovis loaves. Bread was always put on wire trays. We had a long pole with a hook on the end to pull the trays out as these were too far back to reach by hand. Thinking about it now, how we got the cakes and biscuits seems very old fashioned. In the corner of the yard was a brick built building about the size of two 8x6 sheds, where two men worked. One was an elderly gentleman who had worked there forever. We had to stand in line out in the open. If it rained all the confectionery got wet, so we ran to the van as quick as we could. What was really surprising was we would say just what we wanted, for example, six packets of rich tea biscuits, two lemon cakes, six steam puddings and so on, and as the old fellow placed the items asked for on a wooden tray, on a piece of paper he wrote down the prices of each item. What amazed me was he would run up and down the list of prices adding up all the money, he was so fast, if he made a mistake and under charged the rounds man, it was a gain to the rounds man. A slip was given and added to the cost of the bread when we cashed up on Saturday afternoon for the week's goods and handed over the money. All the time I was there, I never knew that man to make a mistake when adding up for the confectionary.

Off we go. To my delight our first stop was the Jolly Tea Pot café, situated in Stechford lane. That was the start of our round in that lane. We had two slices of toast and a cup of tea every morning, and the rounds man always paid. It was a very pleasant job in the summer, not so good in the winter when it rained, trying to keep the bread dry.

I found I had a flair for selling. The more cakes and biscuits we sold, the more bonus we got. Malcolm said his wages had never been so good. I loved selling. By the time I had done one month, we were getting four wooden trays of confectionery every Monday, and we added more items to them through the week. Malcolm thanked me. I was called into the office and praised for my endeavours and given a raise of a shilling. Ok, only a shilling, but it was worth that for the praise I got, as that was a rare event in my life.

I was eventually taken off that round and put with a man called Mr Pratt; his rounds boy had passed out as a rounds man and got his own round. He whispered to me, "I bet you don't last the week with Pratt." He was right, I lasted three days; nothing I did suited him. I tried selling and pushing the confectionery, as I did on my other round, but he told me not to do it as his customers knew what they wanted. Plus, he didn't like my attire. All the rounds boys had a little book in which we put down what we had given each customer – he didn't like that, he wanted me to remember what they had had without writing it down. He got verbally very aggressive. He said, "You work on my round now, not on Malcolm's round." Every hour seemed like a week, he was a horrible man.

On Saturday when the rounds man was collecting the money, all the rounds boys had to deliver to every customer. The rounds man never touched a loaf on that day, he moaned at me nonstop. I never knew all my customers, never mind his; I had only done three days on his round. I went into work late on the Monday morning to make sure he had left the yard; I went to see the manager,

"May I go back to my old round, please? I can't work with Mr Pratt."

"Yes, ok son, I know what he is like, he gives all the rounds boys a hard time. His customers love him – they sing his praises, so we put up with him. Well, all the vans are out now so you can work on the deck today," the manager told me, so I swept up the deck and arranged all the cradles in the bays ready for the returning vans to unload any bread that they hadn't sold. I liked working on the deck. When the vans had all returned and unloaded I saw what I didn't like to see, a man backed up to the deck and threw all the returned bread into the back of his lorry, so I asked him what he did with the bread. He told me each loaf cost him a penny, yes one penny, and this was fed to the pigs as it wasn't allowed to be sold to the public a day later.

I asked Mr Starkey if I could do the job on the deck permanent, but I was refused because it wasn't classed as a job. Mr Pratt's old rounds boy backed onto the deck to unload the returned bread ready for the pig man to collect. After he'd unloaded he turned, saw me, smiled and said, "Told you you wouldn't last the week with Mr Pratt."

I worked there for eight months. Part of my job was to plug the van into the electric ready to be charged up for the next day. Each van had two very big batteries, one each side, underneath they were the length of the van.

As usual I got fed up and handed in my notice. This type of behaviour became the norm for me throughout the rest of my life.

A few years later I went back to the Co-op and became a rounds man. Nothing had changed, the only difference was that I was in charge of and responsible for the money. I much preferred being a rounds boy – no responsibility.

Manor Road Bakery, Stechford, showing the lorries backed on to the deck. The van far right is where I used to plug in the electrics for the batteries to be charged over night.

DONOVANS

Early one morning I had the idea I would go all around the local building sites, so I sat for a while and worked out a route I would take, starting with the nearest first, in the hope I wouldn't have to walk too far. I got to a place called the Atlas, well that's what we called that area because the cinema there was named the Atlas, and the area was Stechford. About a quarter of a mile from my house was a café on the corner of Albert Road, I can't remember the name of it, it was there for years, it's gone now like all the things we wish were still around. I went in there and had three tomato dips, that's bread dipped in the juice of the tomatoes, they were only 2d each, two pence, 6d in total; sixpence, that's all I could afford – all my mates had tomato dips when short of money. With a little food in my stomach, off I set. Just behind the café was a grove of factories. As I was passing them, I thought, could I be locked away all day working in one of those? I pondered on it for a while and thought, well it might be all right; it won't hurt to give it a go. These factories were in Northcote Road, and at the bottom of the grove was a firm that made items out off concrete. I thought I'd try at Stuarts granolithic, but as I passed a factory called Donovans, for reasons I can't explain, I walked into their office and asked if they had any vacancies. The ladies had only just taken off their coats, and I was asked to wait ten minutes. I filled in an application form, and then a foreman whose name was Johnson came to me and asked what type of work I was looking for. "Anything," I replied.

"Are you ok at maths?"

"Not too bad," I replied. Good at maths? I could hardly read; well, all they could do was sack me. I always took chances like that; normally they would just put you on a different job if you weren't any good on the one they employed you for. I was shown all over the factory and shown what they made, which was electric boxes, well all the wiring that went inside them, from six foot tall cabinets to little on off switches, the type with a lever on the side that you pushed up for ‘off’ and down for ‘on’, these items were for factories. It was a family firm, a wonderful atmosphere.

They used thick copper wire bent into shape with a pair of pliers, they used a sheet with all the shapes on it, so they knew the shape was correct, and then it was placed in the cabinet with a nut and a washer, and was fixed into place. The job I was given was a checker; the foreman said I was in charge of seeing the girls and ladies had enough work in their trays so they didn’t need to stop working. They were all on piecework. Using hand presses, they punched out all sorts of electric parts. I had to collect the trays when full, weigh them, write down the amount they had done, put it in my book then hand it to the manager so the ladies money could be worked out. The ladies kept a record of what they did so they could make sure their pay was correct. Working around all those ladies and girls this is, I was thinking to myself, heaven, yes sir, heaven.

The foreman asked, “Are you interested in taking the job?”

“Yes,” I replied.

So I now had a title – Checker. Can you believe it, me with a responsible job? I felt important at that moment in time, I can tell you. This was a learning curve for me; I was what was known at that time as dim, yes, very dim. There were sixteen ladies to look after.

“Start at eight in the morning and bring your cards with you.”

“I have them with me,” I replied.

“Ok, I will take you to the office and you can do the necessary there.” He told me his name and said I will see you in the morning.

The next morning I started rather nervous, in fact very nervous. I had a little office, well a corner with my scales, note book and pencils. I swept up, got a rag and cleaned down the scales and tided up all around what I called my office space – boy I felt important!

The foreman brought Mr Donovan down to show him what I had done; they were well pleased. I had to eat my lunch in my little bit of heaven.

Across the gangway from my scales were all the presses. The lady who worked closest to me was named Valerie; she was a large lady, like my mom was, and I got on so well with her. I explained to her, rather embarrassingly, that I did not know how to weigh and calculate the scales. She looked amazed, "Do you know how many there are in a gross?" she asked me.

"No," I replied. She said she would take me under her wing and very quietly would tell me what to do and how to use the scales properly.

"Don't worry, Dave, I won't tell anyone," she very kindly said. "Dinnertime I will write all the amounts down for you, and if you get stuck just come and see me and I will put you right." I was so relieved.

After a week I was ok, I picked it up and knew how to do the job properly, so I really looked after Val, making out she had done more than she had. If we fiddled too much she would make a note of the work she didn't want paying for that week, and put it down for the next week, which meant she could have an easier week and not have to work so hard. Valerie had a free day every week because I said in the book that she had done that day's quota – well one good turn and all that. It also meant if she had a day off she never lost any money.

I joined the football team; my position was right half. We played every dinnertime at the back of the factory – we were called the Donovan F.C., makes sense I suppose. We played on a Saturday morning. We won the league that year 1960, Mr Donovan was well pleased.

Well, time to move on. I did well there – I lasted about four months. When I left that company outside the sun was shining. I felt I needed to work out in the fresh air instead of a stuffy, dark factory. I was asked if I would still play football for them, which I agreed to do.

STUARTS GRANOLITHICS

This firm was situated in Northcote road off Albert road in the Stechford area of Birmingham, the same road that Donovans was in. I left Donovans to start work with Stuarts, and I was told the firm were moving to Coleshill in six months' time, after their new factory had finished being built. The day I went to ask if they had any vacancies, they had just started building their new factory that very week; the new factory was in Station road Coleshill, in the county of Warwickshire, and they made various items of concrete for the housing market. I walked into the office and asked the manager if they had any vacancies.

"We are looking for a strong young man to do some labouring on our new building site at Coleshill," he said.

"That's ok," I told him, the personnel manager that is.

"Right son, start tomorrow eight thirty," he told me.

"How do I get there?" I asked him.

"By bus son, we will be putting on transport to pick the men up but not for another week, we have only been on the site for three days getting ready for the building to start, which we have done today," he told me.

The buses were every hour but they didn't run to Coleshill from where I lived, so I walked to that site in Coleshill. It took me over an hour and a half, and it was winter time but the days were quite warm – well, they were to me as I didn't feel the cold like most people did – and it had rained the night before. On the first morning I started I didn't do very much work, I was asked to level out a large pile of rubble, well it was called hard core and was crushed up old house bricks, but that was all I did that morning. By lunch time I felt really rough – I had the flu coming on. I had my lunch with the men in the shanty, which is the wooden hut used by the workers to hang up their coats and have their breaks in. I started back on the site after my lunch break, but by this time I was feeling really ill, and after about an hour, maybe a little more, I just could not carry on – it got so bad I couldn't even lift the shovel. I went to see the boss in his office, I knocked on the door and a voice shouted 'enter,' and to my surprise the boss had his trousers around his knees and he was adjusting his pants. There were two other men in there with him and they were laughing – I had no idea why at that time.

"I'm sorry boss, I will have to go home, I – " but before I could finish what I was saying he interrupted me.

"I don't know why they employ people like you, your type shouldn't work around men." I was getting worse by the minute and had no idea at that time what he was trying to say to me – I just wanted to go home. "You are not the type to work for me so I'm letting you go, you can come and collect your wages and your money at the office on Friday."

I was devastated but far too ill to argue or defend myself, and as I left the site I realised what he meant: he thought I was queer, or should I say gay these days. Gay meaning happy, I wasn't very happy and I can tell you no way am I gay, I love the ladies too much. As I started on the long walk home it started to pour with rain, and I was wearing a coat that was too small for me and I couldn't button it up, so I just felt like I was going to die – not that I know what dying is like, but I'm sure you know what I mean. Walking down that country lane where they were building their new factory, there were lots of puddles quite deep all down the lane from all the rain the night before, and they were being made worse because as I walked the rain got really heavy.

What made me feel even worse was a lorry coming towards me just as I got near a very deep puddle – I turned to run away but my legs just wouldn't move fast enough. I felt so weak and the driver in the lorry thought he would have a bit of fun and put his foot down, steered his lorry closer to me and hit that puddle so fast the water rose into the air and came down over me like a tidal wave. Talk about being wet, if I had jumped into a river I would not have been any wetter. I was shivering, my whole body was shaking and I had a terrible headache. It was really hurting me to even walk by this time and I still had about an eight or ten mile walk to reach home. I just wanted to lie down and sleep, and as I walked – more like staggered – I came across a fallen tree. I sat down and tried to regain some of my strength but I was getting worse, and still it poured with rain. I forced myself off the tree and headed for home. I shivered and shook with every step I took and as I reached my house I wasn't sure if I was alive or dead.

As I walked into the back kitchen my mom said, "My word son you look dreadful, get yourself off to bed I will wash those wet clothes." I took off my clothes and just left them where they fell on the bedroom floor. I never even dried myself, I just got straight into bed, and fell asleep as soon as my head touched the pillow. I was asleep for two days and not once did I wake up – my mom said she was thinking of getting the doctor to me as she was very worried. When I finally woke up, boy was I weak, and my mum made me a big fry up for breakfast. It was over a week before I ventured out again. There is one thing I would like to do, and that is see that Forman again and tell him how wrong he was about me, and say it was because I had the flu not because I was queer, bent, gay or whatever…well, that will never happen now.

DONOVANS FOR THE SECOND TIME

So I was sacked from Stuarts Granolithics and the time came for me to be a little cheeky. So with a nice smile I walked into the office of Donovans and knocked on the personnel office window. It slid open, and the office girl recognised me. "Hello David, how are you? How can I help you?"

"Would you ask Mr Johnson if I can have my job back please?" Well if you don't ask, as the saying goes.

It was a good ten minutes before he came out to see me. As he walked through the door I held out my hand with a smile, and said, "Hello, Mr Johnson, how are you?"

"So you want your job back do you?"

"Yes please," I replied.

He smiled and very sarcastically said, "So your sandcastles fell down, did they?"

I laughed, hoping it would keep him in a good mood. I told a white lie, I said I missed working there {truth is I don't like working anywhere, well there was one job I did love working at, that was Kunzles).

"I can't offer you your old job back, would you like to work on the big cabinets?"

"I would love to do that, Mr Johnson," and I meant it, I even thought to myself, I'm going to stay here till I retire (I'm not sure who was the biggest fool – me or my mind!).

I started the next day. The section was on the other side of the factory from the ladies on the presses. The big cabinets had a printed panel already fixed inside them, with a pair of pliers, I bent the copper wire to the shape printed on the board and placed it on the bolts sticking out of the panel; with a nut and a washer I bolted it in place. The charge hand over that section kept an eye on me for a short time.

"I see you have the hang of it, now you will be ok," he said at the end of the first week – I was well into it.

I found in life if you have a go it might turn out all right, nothing lost if it doesn't. When all the copper wire was in situ it looked really nice, seeing all the electric circuits together to me looked like a piece of art. I always imagined it in a beautiful gold frame as a piece of art.

As usual I started to get bored, and I was late a few times. One time I was late I went to the office, that's what you had to do when you were late. One of the office staff went to Mr Johnson, told him I was late and asked if I could start work. The answer I received was, "Tell Mr P to have the rest of the day off," so I wasn't allowed in that day.

I got a telling off the next day. I said, "Better late than never," and he replied, "Better never late." I've never forgotten that. I tried to overcome the boredom but it got the better of me, so I handed in my notice.

The one thing I did really miss was my girlfriend. She left her job at Barrows Stores in town and got a job in the office at Donovans to be near me; I never knew she did that till one Monday dinnertime when she came and sat with me; I was shocked, I can tell you, what a lovely thing for a person to do. We got married on the 23rd December 1961, aged eighteen (poor girl). Wonderful memories.

F- LINE AND CO

When I started at this factory I was so surprised at how old fashioned it was; it was situated near the Birmingham city centre, in Staniforth Street. The methods used there were so old fashioned it opened one's eyes to think in these days of modern technology, or should I say in those days, these machines were still being used, mind you even when I was young I loved the past, that's what I do, live in the past. Any road up, the machines were being driven by leather belts. It was a very interesting building, cubby holes, passage ways, hidey holes everywhere; honestly if I hadn't known better I could have thought I was working in the Dickensian times. Brick walls, whitewashed, hanging in dust and cobwebs, nails knocked in the joints between the bricks with all sorts of things hanging on them, some of those items hanging on those nails looked like they had been there five hundred years or more. I used to grease the pulleys that drove the leather belts that made the machines work. I was taught how to repair the belts when they broke, it was fascinating to me, learning the old fashioned way of working and repairing items that had been used since the year dot, well the early eighteen hundreds I would imagine. It was much harder than it looked getting things level, and make do and mend, nothing at that firm was wasted, they were very frugal. I thought they were mean at that time when I worked for them, I can see now I'm older that every penny counted.

The room that really fascinated me was the degreasing room; this room had sacks of sawdust in there, which was put in wooden barrels which were turning at an angle with the items to be degreased in them, usually spanners or wheels for roller skates, all metal wheels. This method worked very well but it made a deafening noise as the barrels turned and the metal objects hit each other. Whatever was put in the barrels came out very shiny, it was amazing. The trouble was when working in the degreasing room it turned out the sawdust affected my eyes, I started to suffer with sties on my eyes. My doctor told me not to work in the sawdust, and I took a note from the doctor explaining the problem. I felt like a little school boy taking a note from my mommy. The boss was ok about it; he asked me if I wanted to be a tool setter. "Very much, thank you, sir." I always said 'sir' when I was creeping.

I really enjoyed learning something new. I was shown how to sharpen drills, set presses, how to grind down a press punch when it went blunt. He was so pleased with my work he put me in charge of six presses. That was funny; the six ladies always wanted the best jobs that brought them better wages, and I tried to be fair, but as they say, you can't please them all. One lady started to bring me sweets, one lady fruit, and one, well let's say she tried to touch where the sweets and fruit never touched. It got so I was worried about walking past her. Today she wouldn't be so lucky – I'm not so innocent now.

One day I was setting up a press for punching out blanks for spanners, the shape that came out looked like dogs bones. "Ok Ann, you can go on this press now." I'm not sure why I remember her name. After about eight or ten minutes of her working on the press I heard such a bang, I ran to see what had happened. Poor Ann was in tears, I calmed her down and told to go and have a cup of tea. I had forgotten to tighten the bed down, what a terrible mistake it was, a new punch and it had a chunk out of it. I very quickly put it on the grinder and sharpened it back up. I must have ground five years worth of work off it, I set it up as quickly as I could and the boss never knew it had happened. I put Ann back on it and told her it was an old bed and it had a crack in it so I had replaced it with a new one. She was ok, and then I booked her extra work so she didn't lose any money. I never did make a mistake like that again, I checked twice every time I set up a press.

Next day I was talking to the boss and he said, "I like your time keeping and your work is good. About six weeks after that I handed in my notice; new horizons here I come. I have to say, it was bad news for any firm to take me on.

Putting the metal stamped out shapes into the barrels with sawdust shovelled in – all the grease was removed, they came out really shiny.

KUNZLES

It was one of those days I didn't care if I got a job or not, I suppose it was because I wasn't responsible enough, I don't know. I was walking down Garrets Green Lane, hands in pockets, not a care in the world, you would have thought not caring that I was rich or I had lots of money, no way, I hadn't a penny to my name. When I saw the Kunzles factory, I thought, well it won't hurt to try; I will ask if there are any jobs going. Just as I was about to walk down the slope a gentleman standing at the foot of it said to me, "Are you looking for a job, son?"

"Yeah," I said, thinking he was a worker there.

He said, "If they say there are no vacancies, tell them they want a worker in the warehouse in Tyseley."

So I knocked on the sliding glass window and asked if they had any vacancies. I was told no. I told them what the man at the top of the slope had said, that there was one at Tyseley. Well, out came the personnel officer, who said I could have the job as a warehouse hand. The wages were £8 per week and I was to wait at the top of the slope for him and he would take me in his car, show me the way and the job. As I approached the gentleman who was still standing at the top of the slope, he said "Did you get it?"

"Yes, sir." He smiled and I thanked him. He turned out to be Mr Kunzle junior himself.

The warehouse was on the side of the canal. I thought, yes this looks ok. Only four men worked there; one did all the export packing, his name was Michael, he had worked there a few years; the other three, Howard the boss, and Bill and Phillip the warehouse hands, all had worked for Kunzles since they were fourteen it turned out. I was told Mr Kunzle created that position for me – I must have looked very down to him; what a kind thing to do. The warehouse was rented off the British Waterways, it was off the road called Wharfdale road. I was taken back to the office and filled in all the forms; I felt good at that moment in time, funny really, I didn't care before if I got a job or not, now I felt pleased.

The next morning I caught two buses to get there. As I walked from the bus I was lost, I just could not remember where the warehouse was. I had my lunch in a paper carrier, it was raining, I still only owned a coat that was too small for me so I couldn't fasten it up, or hide my lunch under it. The carrier fell apart and to be honest so did I. I threw my lunch in a rubbish bin and thought, that's it, to hell with the job; I'm going home – I was very wet by this time. As I turned to walk to the bus stop I noticed a phone box; I rang the operator, got Kunzles phone number, asked them where the warehouse was, and explained the problem – they were very understanding.

When I arrived the men told me to take it easy and to dry my coat by the heater. Come dinnertime they shared their food with me. I liked that day; after all, my job was to load all the lorries that came in with bundles of cardboard boxes, and of course to unload them. The printed boxes that they put the cakes into for the shops were for their famous cakes called showboats, a chocolate case filled with cream and decorated. I have a very sweet tooth but I just could not eat those cakes. The cardboard boxes had codes on them so we knew what size to send back to the factory – ax ½ ax and many more funny codes like that.

When it was quiet they put me to work in the export department, I loved it in there. I had to use silver foil with a film of plastic coating on it, this I used to wrap up boxes of chocolates, then with a soldering iron, I sealed all the folds I had made. I can smell that melting plastic now as I type. Then with the right size wooden crate, I lined it with tar paper, placed the tin foil wrapped chocolates in the crate, I then put wood shavings or wood wool as we called it, all around the parcel for further protection. I then nailed on the lid and with a stencil I stencilled on the name and the destination. I then put four steel bands around the case so no one could lift the lid. Those chocolates went all around the world, I loved that job.

After a few months of working there I got married on the 23rd December 1961, it was going to be the week before, but Irene's dad asked if we would change it to the week after as his two sons and Irene's young sister were booked at his firm's Christmas party on the 16th. That week leading up to the 16th I got a throat infection, I could

Ladies packing marshmallows

The export department. I'm packing chocolates in foil with plastic coating and sealing it before I pack it in wooden cases

not even swallow or say a word, so if Irene's dad hadn't have asked us to change the date I could not have got married, I could not have said I will. The good Lord smiled on us that year that's for sure. It was a very bitter cold day; on the 23rd December 1961 I was warm with love though.

On my return to work after Christmas it was still very cold and icy. I repaired the bike I had made up from the tip all those years before but my then wife didn't want me to go to work on my bike. "Don't worry," I said, "I will be fine; anyway we can't afford the bus fares." We had five shillings, that's all we had, 5/- between us – nothing in the bank. I had never had a bank book at that time in my life, sounds like I'm old, I was only eighteen. Any road up, I cycled through Shard End, Lea village, through the Mackadown. When I got to the Meadway I cut through the housing estate I did a right hand turn – the bike went right, I went left, and my bike stopped in the middle of the road. As I tried to get up I kept slipping back down, the road was a sheet of ice and it was on a hill. A car turned the corner, all his windows were iced up, and all he had to see out of was a little round circle. His face was pressed up to the windscreen so he could see where he was going. He spotted my bike, and skidded all over the place. That's it, I thought, he will squash my bike. He stopped about two inches from it, so I avoided that road till all the snow and frost had gone.

As I was now married and only earning £8 it wasn't enough for us to live on. I had done one year and I loved the job, I never had a day off all the time I was there – when the day ended I never wanted to go home, it was a fantastic place to work for, but we needed money to live so I got a job just around the corner at a bed factory called Slumberland. My wages were doubled, £16 per week, so very reluctantly I left. I never felt that way ever again about any of the jobs I had, and as you will see, I had many.

SLUMBERLAND

After leaving Kunzles, now that job I loved but the pay was low, I started working for a bed company known as Slumberland. At Kunzles my wages were eight pounds a week, but I had just got married so I needed more money. Slumberland started me on at sixteen pounds a week, which doubled my wages from my last job. In those days you didn't get full wages until you were twenty one, they considered that to be the coming of age.

Slumberland was just around the corner from the warehouse that I worked in for Kunzles, that was Wharfdale Road, Tyseley; Slumberland was in Kings Road, Tyseley. I told my then wife I had got a new job with double the money, but she wasn't surprised, I had had a few jobs, even at the tender age of eighteen. I rode that old bike that I had made up from the tip to work, so I never had to pay out any bus fares.

I reported to a Mr Beddows, he had the right name to work at a bed factory; well it amused me at the time. I hadn't a clue what job they were going to give to me; I was taken all around the factory and shown all the different departments. "Well, young man, I think seeing how you are a big fellow I will put you loading the lorries with the bed springs." Oh, good, I thought, I will be working outside. Just inside the bay was a big vertical machine; twelve completed mattress springs were placed in that machine and squeezed together, then with pieces of wire threaded through them and twisted the springs were easier to move as one lot. My job then was with another helper, we would wheel them to the lorry then with hooks we dragged them on to the lorry – it was very heavy work, by the time we had loaded the lorry we knew we had done it. I think those springs were sold to other companies because they hadn't the machinery to make the springs. When the lorry pulled away we had sometimes a little breathing space. I used to go all round the different departments, it was fascinating to watch the different operations, plus I used to help myself to the different size screws, in those days screws were expensive. I loved to learn about different things in life, maybe that's why I've had so many jobs.

When no lorries were expected I had to sweep up the yard and drive a forklift truck. I didn't drive till I was twenty but I picked up driving that forklift with no bother, another string to my bow I thought at that time. (I've thrown that bloody bow away now, ha, ha!)

If you worked over, the wages officer always went round asking the reason why and you had to explain, overtime was a rare happening in the week but one was expected to work Saturday mornings. One evening I was messing with my push bike doing a puncture, so I thought I would be clever and clock out at fifteen minutes after five, the next afternoon the wages officer came to me and hit the roof! I was accused of fraud, threatened with the sack and court, and all for fifteen minutes. The foreman was called and I explained about the bike and said I forgot about clocking out. The foreman was asked if I was any good or should I be sacked; he stuck up for me so I was told never to let it happen again – as if I would after all that!

Saturday came; it was my first anniversary so I asked Mr Beddows if I could go early so I could go up town to get my wife a silver bracelet she had asked for specially. It was all hearts joined together; it cost thirteen shillings and sixpence 13/6. "Yes, ok, seeing how it's your anniversary. I will clock you out at twelve midday." So that was done. It was H.Samuel's last one as well. Every year after that I bought a silver charm for our anniversary, which she put on the bracelet.

While I worked there I got a new cot mattress for my new son at only a third of the price.

One day out of the blue, and it wasn't planned, I handed in my notice. Well I got fed up. You are irresponsible, I hear you say; yes, I was, I would have to agree with you there; to be honest I think I still am.

CONCENTRIC

This firm was based in the Erdington area of Birmingham, on the Tyburn Road, just up the road from where Spaghetti Junction is now. They made transmission parts for cars. If that firm was around today they would be had up by the health and safety body.

I was on a milling machine, milling parts that were obsolete, for old cars, classics they call them now. Talk about going back in time, if you were seen talking to anyone the foreman told you off, and you even had to tell them when you needed the loo; it was like being back at school.

One afternoon I was told to go upstairs to work, to go on a drilling machine. There were lots of machines and lots of women working up there – now that I didn't mind. As you got to the top of the stairs the room was filled with oil mist from floor to ceiling. "Ain't that bad for you?" I asked the foreman.

"It ain't done me any harm, as it? I've been here for years."

I was breathing that oil mist in all afternoon; I only worked in there that once I'm glad to say. I wonder if those ladies health suffered in later years. They no longer use that building, I wonder if they moved somewhere else or if they went bust. I only lasted a couple of months there, now there is a surprise, eh?

On the machine opposite mine worked an old school chum, his name was Michael and he was telling me he had a moped for sale and would I be interested in buying it as he knew I had no transport. As I was talking to him the foreman spotted us and shouted, "Stop talking and get back to your machine." I'm a married man with a child, I thought to myself, I'm not at school now; I will not be spoken to like a child. A few days after, I did buy the moped and travelled to work on it. One lunch time I thought I would go out for a ride on this lovely new toy, I got a bit carried away and ended up at my cousin's house in Aston. Needless to say, that afternoon I did not return to work. Next morning I was asked what had happened to me the previous afternoon. I told the foreman a lie, that I had got lost and couldn't find my way back, to which the foreman said," Aston is only down the road."

"I know," I said to him, "but I don't know this area that well."

He just kept moaning at me, so I told him to, "Lick em on – I'm off."

So my dear wife once again went short of money. Writing this I can see just how much of an idiot I was, yes, and truly irresponsible, I can see it now, I couldn't then.

TWO BUILDING FIRMS

On A very cold and frosty morning I went to the then closed down Castle Bromwich aerodrome; they had just about started what we now know as the Castle Vale housing estate; Bryant's, if my memory serves me right were the builders. I went to the site agent's office and made enquiries about a job.

"I need a few labourers, are you interested in that?" the foreman asked me.

"Oh yes," I replied.

"Have you got your cards with you?"

"Yes," I replied.

"Oh good, that makes a change. I've been told not to start anyone on without their cards; hand them in to the office then see the store man."

Office? It was a little shed. I did what was asked of me and went to the stores, and I was given a second hand pair of wellies, a pick and a shovel. Did you know every time a building firm set up a new site whoever started on that site got a pair of Wellingtons that some other person had worn before – three or four different people could have worn those same Wellingtons, many hours of people's sweaty feet in them, and now I was wearing them. What I did was to say they were leaking. I did that till I got a new pair; mind you that didn't work every time. Any road up, all building sites in those days did that, I wonder if they still do. So I was taken to the very first foundation being dug out by hand, yes by hand, we have come along a bit since then, they now have mechanical diggers. I went into the hole where six Irish men were swinging their pick axes to loosen the soil then shovel it out. As I said, it was a very cold frost bitten morning. I swung my pick at what I thought was a powerful swing, but on contact with the soil it made a little dent in the ground. Right, I thought, I will show you who the master is. I swung that pick with every ounce of strength I had and to my surprise another little dent. There was a Polish ganger walking round this trench, well foundation, shouting come on, come on we have to get this done today! I never liked working under those conditions. I was working on the first foundation to be dug out on the Castle Vale estate. I picked up my shovel, threw it out of that hole, the pick followed it, and I followed them both. "What do you think you are doing?" I heard a voice shout after me.

Turning around I just shouted, "I'm off!" I handed my wellies, pick and shovel back to the store man, then into the office I went. "I've packed it in."

The young man looked at his watch and in a shocked voice he said, "What's the matter?"

I told him, "I don't like people shouting out orders."

"I don't know how much to pay you," the surprised looking pay clerk said.

"Don't worry about that," I replied, "just give me my cards back."

So that was that. I walked across the road to another building firm known as Wimpey's, I was told this means we import more paddies every year – an Irishman told me that; I've never known if he was joking or not, I've never ever tried to find out. This building firm Wimpey's was on the Chester Road, it was their main office. I went to the reception and asked if there were any vacancies. I was taken to the yard foreman.

"Yes I could do with a lad to work in the yard, would that be ok for you?"

"Yes sir," I replied with enthusiasm.

"Right, go to the stores, get a donkey jacket and a pair of gloves and a scraper then report back to me."

I did what he asked. He said, "See those two silos, go and scrape all the concrete off them, sand them down then go to the stores and get a gallon tin of yellow paint and paint them."

Silos are filled with cement, when a lever is pulled it releases a measured amount of cement to be used in the concrete. It was a great job, easy, not like digging holes, and I had a nice warm donkey jacket to wear. I worked hard and the foreman was very pleased with me.

I was the only Brummie there in that yard at that time. I was driving the dumpers moving items, all sorts of things, it was great. I was alone, the men only talked to me if they had to. One morning a boy straight from Ireland was put to work along side of me, he was very nice, well brought up, excellent manners, he put me to shame. We got on so well I was asked to look after him. Every now and again he took out his rosary beads. His name was Michael. Once he found his feet he got in with the other Irish men and he started to work alongside them, so once again I was alone.

Three and a half months passed and I went to see the foreman – he was a very nice man, very easy to talk to and he treated me very well.

"I wish to hand in my notice," I told him.

"Oh dear, are you sure, Dave?" he said. "Now the weather is better it will be much easier in the yard from here on in."

"Thank you," I said, "but I want a change."

"Ok, son, if you ever decide to come back you, can have your job back."

Well, on my travels once again; it was always an adventure to me to start a new job.

MARSH AND BAXTER'S

Marsh and Baxter's, now this was a different type of job altogether. I was taken on for two weeks; this trial period was to see if I was any good. I was taken all around the factory by the supervisor to see all the different operations from slaughtering the pigs, to the curing of bacon and making lard – it was a fascinating and wonderful experience, so different to what I had ever done. I found the slaughtering of the pigs a little disturbing being an animal lover, so I kept well away from that department.

I was shown into the lard room. "This is where you will be working; what do you think?"

"Yes I would like to work in here," I told the supervisor.

"That's fine, we start at six am. I know it's early but we have had to do it that way because of the car factory down the road, it was chaos when we knocked off at the same time as them so we start early and finish early." That was a body blow to me; I found getting up in the mornings a real problem, plus I hated going to work. "Are you still wanting the job, son, you look a little doubtful?"

"No I'm ok with it. I look forward to learning all about this side of life, it's all new to me," I told him.

"That's what we like to hear at Marsh and Baxter's," he said. "Right, see you in the morning then."

The next morning I was given a pair of white Wellingtons, two white coats and an apron, and a little cap – the cap of course was to prevent hair getting into the lard. They had a room to get changed in. No matches, cigarettes or food of any kind was allowed in the abattoir – or slaughter house to anyone who is like me and had never heard the word abattoir – well anywhere inside the factory. The changing room was across the yard from the factory. I was taken to see the foreman of the lard room, a quiet spoken man, nice to work with, John was his name. The vat where the lard was refined was sunk on a lower floor; it was two levels, top floor then down six steps to the bottom floor. The vat was round and six foot across and five foot deep. The top of the vat was level with the top floor; there was a rail right across the top floor, when leaning over it the boiling lard could be viewed. It got to twice the heat of boiling point, so I was told. My job was to fetch the trolleys full of the pig skins with lots of fat on them, throw them in to a very big mincer that was fixed over the vat, and then fill the vat with water that was very hot. Then the foreman turned on the steam pipe which heated the vat to twice the heat of boiling point; this melted the fat off the skin, which turned to lard – there was a big paddle turning all the time it was boiling. The foreman set a timer so he knew when to turn off the steam, and we piped the lard into tins which were already in the fridge, one pound tins that customers bought after it had been delivered to the shops, and six pounds tins which some shop keepers had delivered like this and then they would cut, weigh and wrap the amount the customer had asked for.

First thing every morning when the vat was full and rendering, me and the other lad would get the tins from the fridge that we had filled the day before, bang them upside down on a steel table, then wrap them in the greaseproof paper. We had a trolley with a wheel on each corner, the sides were two foot deep and six foot long made of aluminium, and very light. The trays could be taken off the wheels, they were stackable, and we always had two trays. When we had filled the top tray with the lard we had just wrapped – we always timed it so the deck foreman went to have his breakfast, this left the deck and the fridge deserted – we would empty the top tin fast as the bottom one never had anything in it, and we could hide whatever we wanted in the bottom one – we always had a frozen chicken – when back in the lard room we tied a piece of string to the chicken, put it in the vat and it cooked in no time flat; we did that every day and it tasted good. One day it fell off the string and got rendered down with the lard. When the vat was emptied it left the scratchings, we shovelled them in to sacks, and they were then sold to a firm who salted them and put them in little bags, the type you always see in pubs.

One day I pushed a trolley load of skins that had been left or forgotten about, and as I was throwing it into the mincer I was looking at the end seeing all the strings of meat coming out, the patterns fascinated me. When I looked into the trolley, to see how much skin was left to throw

Burning the hairs off the pigs then scrubbing them clean before they are dipped in boiling water

Taking the warpped lard to the deck fridge so it can be put on the lorries to be delivered to the shops for sale

in, I could not believe what I was looking at – thousands of maggots! I had been mincing up maggots by the thousands, how long that trolley of skin had been there I have no idea. When I say thousands that is no exaggeration, I had minced over half the trolley load, so I went to the hygiene man who looked and said, "I will take a sample out of the vat when it's at its top heat." So I was told not to put anymore in to the vat but we poured it into the tins as normal. Next morning we wrapped it and it went to the shops as normal. Two days later the hygiene man came up to me and said, "That sample I took hasn't bred any bacteria."

"It's a bit late now," I said, "it's gone to the shops and sold by now."

So I told my wife, "Don't buy any Marsh and Baxter's lard, it's rendered down maggots." They say what the eyes don't see – how true that is.

When we cleaned down we used a very hot steam gun, it made the room spotless. It was like a skating rink, with a push off the walls we could slide right across the room with no trouble.

As per usual, after three months I handed in my notice, time to move on. Mind you, I did go to see the boss and said, "I have changed my mind; can I stay?"

"All right," he said. But the next morning I was half an hour late and he told me he had changed his mind and said I wasn't wanted any more. Do you know I was shocked he made me leave, I thought at the time, what a cheek, he doesn't deserve to have me work for him anyway. He did that firm a favour did he not?

REMPLOY

Remploy, in Garrets Green Lane, is a firm mostly for the disabled; why not, I thought it might be an interesting job. So into the office I went. A very pretty young lady slid back a glass window, I always remember a pretty young lady. "Can I help you young man?" she asked.

"Have you any vacancies please?" I asked, half hoping she would reply with those words I loved to hear, 'no sorry'. I hated work, especially inside a factory. "Please wait a moment, I will ask the personnel manager," she replied.

A very smartly dressed gentleman came out and said, "Are you looking for employment?"

"Yes sir," I replied.

"We need a charge hand, would you be interested?"

"Yes sir, what are the wages."

I can't remember what he told me but I do remember it was fantastic money for a youngster. "Are you interested?" he asked again.

"Oh yes," I told him.

"Ok, good," he said to me, "could you start tomorrow?"

"Yes, no problem," I replied.

"Good. Wait there, I will tell Mr (I can't remember his name) he is the boss; he will bring the forms to you for you to fill in."

This is too good to be true, I was thinking to myself, and so it was. In walked the boss and he took one look at me and said, "I'm sorry, son, I can't offer you the job Roy offered you, he gets carried away sometimes, I can offer you a job as a checker, checking the work that the workers produce and weighing items they are pressing out on the hand presses, but the wages are less than half of the wages that were offered you in the first place. However, you can get advancements if you prove your worth." What the wages were I can't remember, but I accepted the job and started the next day.

I had no idea what any of the items I was weighing were for, and I wasn't really interested. The building was full of disabled workers but I do remember a lad who wasn't disabled who just constantly chatted up the young girls and the older ladies. I tried hard to like that job, but after a few days I hated it so much; I was bored stiff. So after only two and a half weeks I handed in my notice and it was back on the building sites for me...

HUMPHREYS AND GLASGOW

Humphreys and Glasgow was a firm that were based in the north of the country, Yorkshire or Lancashire, I really can't remember. I was earning thirty pounds a week when most people were only earning twelve to fifteen pounds a week. This company's main role was boiler work.

I started work with this firm on a Monday morning, and travelled by coach with my brother in-law, Thomas White, who had got me the job. We caught the coach every morning at 7.15 to Hams Hall Power Station where I was labouring for this company. It was the easiest job I've ever had. We were carrying fire bricks, and those bricks weighed nothing at all. We also mixed the fire clay, which was really easy. I got there a little early each morning to load up the boilers with the fire bricks and the fire clay, and the rest of the day was really easy; about every two hours I would take a few bricks and some clay up to the brickies and then I just dossed about. Sometimes I would get on a dumper and race the regular dumper driver around the site – it's a wonder we weren't sacked!

One afternoon the ganger called me and said, "Come with me Dave, I've got a nice easy job for you." There had been a load of insulation rolls delivered, and he asked me to take them into a shed and stack them. They were made from fibre glass wool, I had never heard of this wool before. I made that job last all afternoon, this is money for old rope, I thought to myself – then the itching started. I did all that throwing around without a mask, which as we all know now, fibre glass can be lethal to our lungs; I wonder if it will affect my lungs when I'm old, ha ha, I'm 67 years old now. I know I am old; mind you, I'm still very active; well I'm slowing down a little nowadays...

When the cement lorry arrived with a few hundred bags of cement, the work force disappeared; the bags in those days weighed one hundred weight each; you knew you had earned your money when the lorry was empty.

The first morning I started work for that company, as we arrived in the coach it was like a bombed building site – someone in the night had set fire to all the shanties, or should I say large sheds. All the workers made a claim for a pair of wellies, a donkey jacket, coats, shoes, boots and many other items. I was standing by the site foreman, he was laughing and he said, “Those shanties wouldn’t hold that amount of gear!” In groups they were taken to the town and they picked up the items they said they had lost in the fire, it really was the best paid job ever.

The boss asked me to stay on and travel around the country with the firm; all the regular work force lived in caravans with their families and travelled with the firm – that was their lives. I declined his offer even though he offered me a new caravan and a lorry to tow it with. A week later I handed in my notice; he tried to talk me out of leaving but I left anyway. Why I get bored so quickly I have no idea, maybe I am lazy.

REDCROFTS TIMBERYARD

This firm is situated in the Castle Bromwich area of Birmingham where it still is to this very day. They sold and delivered all types of building materials, and I visited this yard to purchase one hundred weight of sand when I spotted the notice for a driver. Why not, I thought, if I need any materials for my house I would get employees discount, so I saw Mrs Phillips who was the owner along with her husband; they hadn't been trading long. I was shown around the yard and the saw mill by Mr Phillips.

The manager at that time was a man named Terry; I didn't like him at all. Well, I got the job. I was delivering all around Birmingham; the areas I mostly delivered to were Tile Cross, Castle Bromwich, Lea Village, Shard End, Coleshill and Coventry, in fact anywhere that I was told to go to. It was an easy job most of the time; I used to shovel the sand onto the lorry, seven shovels to the hundred weight. Yes it was all shovel work in those days, that has always stuck in my mind, seven shovels for one hundred weight. When two tons of sand was ordered that was a lot of shovelling. The bags of cement were in hundred weights, that weight wasn't a problem for me at the time; it would be a different story now I might tell you. I think it was all the bags of coal I carried as a child that built up my muscles, well it earned me pocket money, carrying coal I mean, not driving a lorry. (Oh I don't know though ha, ha!) Mind you, those 3x2 paving slabs gave me a problem.

One day I hadn't any deliveries to make so I was asked if I would work in the sawmill, I was delighted – I love wood and the smell of it. The pitch pine when cut was my favourite wood, when cut it gave off a perfume second to none; I used to sniff the off cuts like I was addicted to it, I even cut the off cuts up in to fire wood just so I could smell the wonderful aroma it gave off. I worked on all the machines, but the planing machine I liked the best; I was even allowed to serve customers from time to time – what's so special about that? I hear you say. If you left school as illiterate as I was, you would understand,

Redcrofts Timber and Building Materials Yard

every little step in life, like serving a customer, to me was a great achievement; it didn't come easy, I really had to workhard at life to make things work.

I worked alongside a young lad who had just started there, he was fresh out of school, Malcolm was his name and to this very day he is still there, he now is the manager of that sawmill. I just can't imagine working in the same place for all those years, that ain't me, that's for sure.

Next to Redcrofts was a club called The Rob Roy where many stars stayed, such as Cliff Richard, on their way to venues; previous to this it was run as a nursing home for many years. The owner of Redcrofts ran this as a club. I remember seeing Cliff Richard's photo on the wall. I asked Mr Phillips if I could help to knock the wall down. I helped to put in an R.S.J. but for the life of me I can't remember what they used that club for after it was finished, but what I do remember was when Barrows store closed down Mr Phillips bought all the carpets that were in their restaurant, I went and took it up, and the stair carpet. I have no idea where he used it in the club; I would imagine it was a sad day to see Barrows in such a mess with people tearing things apart. When I first met my wife who was my girlfriend at that time, she worked there as a junior clerk for a lady named Miss Lycett, who had worked there forever. I sat in that restaurant a few times while waiting for my lovely girlfriend, but it always seemed too posh for me. I drove back to the yard with all the carpets and I carried them into that Rob Roy club because it was empty, then back to my deliveries. After the Rob Roy club the name was changed to the Bel Air then the Chesterfield Night Club and the Westbank Club and it was demolished around 1977 and purchased by M.F.I. which has since been sold and is now owned by Aldi and Halfords.

The yard manager, Terry, I just could not get on with at all, so I knew I wouldn't last there. Saturdays I worked in the saw mill till I had a delivery to make. I made some terrible errors when cutting the timber. One error I remember was a customer asked for a piece of pine six feet long by two inches wide and a half inch thick. I got a long plank of pine, cut a strip off it, planed it to size, then cut it to two foot in length, I have no idea why I did that, I covered up that mistake and cut another piece. I did learn a lot about timber and the building trade while I worked there though.

There was one incident I must tell you about. A customer phoned up complaining they hadn't had their delivery – it had been forgotten by the manager so Mrs Phillips asked me to do three deliveries after closing time. I agreed; they were C.O. D. cash on delivery, I did the deliveries, when I got back I knocked on the then bungalow (it's been demolished now and made into a car park) and Mr Phillips came to the door. I gave him the delivery notes and the money, and he pushed a ten shilling note in my top pocket and said, "There you are, Dave, have a drink on me." I thanked him and went home.

The next morning Mrs Phillips told me in a stern voice, "I was ten shillings short in the money." I explained that Mr Phillips had given me the ten shillings and said have a drink on me. She shouted at me and said I shouldn't have taken it and I was not to take any money off him again. I heard her telling him off as well; she was the boss and the driving force in that business. I must add though, a good boss to work for.

No matter how hard you worked it was never good enough for the yard manager. He had no idea how to run a team, so one day I told him to lick em on – I'm off. Not long after that he was sacked. Over the years I have used that firm to buy many items of building materials. Actually I do now from time to time.

M. I. C.

M. I. C. – Midland Industrial Cleaning. I worked casual for this firm many times at different factories all around Birmingham over the years. The work varied quite a lot; this firm stripped, cleaned and polished floors, even polished office furniture, swept up roads, cleaned out acid pits, you name it, if it needed cleaning they would do it, it was a fascinating job.

My younger brother, John, had his cards in with them for a while, but I worked for them cash in hand on a daily basis; if the job was for a couple of weeks or so, they paid me weekly.

One time I worked at King Street in Hockley at the Lucas factory. It was in a room that was air pressured, and as you opened the door there was a very strong wind that came at you. The reason for this was to keep out the dust as they did the sealed head lamps in there for the cars, so no dust could be allowed to get into those lamps. I used Kex mops; I constantly pushed that dry mop around that floor, I wasn't allowed to lift it, it had to be kept flat on the floor. Those mops were about three foot long and about ten to twelve inches wide.

It was only ladies working in that room, and they just loved to embarrass me and make me blush, they were quite naughty at times, one or two were even very rude. I wish it was these days, at my age I would surely make them follow through with their comments – shame I was so young, ha, ha. After working in that room we went outside, my brother John, his co worker and I, and we swept the roads all round that factory.

Some time later I went to Shirley, Lucas's had a works there where they painted the starter motors bodies and other items mostly black. Me and John cleaned the spray paint booths. I worked all the weekend for five pounds and was grateful for that little extra money.

Across the road were the laboratories for Lucas; we worked in there cleaning the stairs, which was such a waste of time as we were cleaning them with liquid polish. There were dozens of people walking up and down every minute of the day; how were we supposed to polish stairs while this was going on? Trouble was we weren't allowed to go in there at night. The windows were cleaned inside and outside from cradles; they had a special team for that job, I would have done it if I had been asked.

At one stage I was given a van to pick up all the men in the mornings; I used it to run my family around, well it was a perk as the saying goes. We all had some cleaning items to take home, with the boss's permission, of course. I did so many different jobs for that company, always cash in hand, and I really enjoyed the variety of jobs and travelling all over the country. I was asked many times if I would go on the cards for them, I always refused, if I had been on the cards I wouldn't have been able to take as many liberties as I did; they say variety is the spice of life – I certainly had a lot of that spice.

BRYANTS

Working on a Bryant's site in the Birmingham area that was once a horse racing course known as Bromford Racing Course (which is now a housing estate) I was a general dogsbody driving the dumpers, running the hoist on the twenty story block of flats, taking all the materials such as bricks, mortar and timber. The hoist was driven by a diesel engine known as a Lister; the drawback to driving that hoist was there were no telephones or bells to let me know when one of the many workers wanted to use the hoist, so to attract my attention they would throw certain items to hit my hard hat – it was very dangerous, if I looked at the wrong moment I could have lost an eye. I did complain to the site agent about the dangers but nothing was ever done to change how that hoist was operated; in those days they got away with health and safety regulations.

There is one time I remember well. I had sent the hoist up to the ninth floor so one of the lads could put a barrow full of rubbish onto it. I thought I heard him shout "OK, Dave," but it wasn't him shouting, it was someone fooling about, so I started to lower the hoist. Unfortunately he had only pushed the wheelbarrow half way onto the hoist, but luck was on his side as he managed to jump back onto the scaffolding, one hand holding on to a scaffold bar and one leg dangling in mid air. The wheelbarrow fell backwards down the gap at the back of the hoist and fell to earth at what seemed like a hundred miles an hour! House bricks, dust, pieces of timber, even lumps of concrete came raining down hitting the scaffolding on its way down, forcing it to fly about twenty yards across the site. I shouted "Take cover!" as I tried to escape the flying debris. The wheelbarrow hit the ground and it seemed to be following me as I was running to avoid getting hurt. The site agent saw what had happened, came over to me and started to shout; I soon put him in his place. I told him where to stick his hoist, and with a red face he got off his soap box and in a calm voice he asked me if I wouldn't mind going around the site with a wheelbarrow and picking up all the rubbish – he even said please! I had to do this with a new wheelbarrow, I might add, the barrow that had fallen was unrecognisable as a wheelbarrow.

It was coming up to dinnertime, about five to one, when I was stopped by a little Irish man, it turned out he was the scaffolding foreman. "I have seen the site agent about you," he said to me. "I told him I want you to work for me scaffolding, and if you agree I will give you scaffolder's rate of pay."

"Yes, I agree," I said to him with no hesitation. Those words, more pay, was music to my ears.

"OK, start after dinner." Well to be honest I got a little big headed, well I was still young.

The foreman handed me a belt with all the tools hanging off it. I swaggered to the hut (known to building site workers as shanty) for my dinner with my brother in law Tom, who worked on the same site. The look on Tom's face when he saw me walk into the shanty with my belt of tools! "What are you doing with that belt of tools Dave?" he enquired.

Chest out, I proudly replied, "I'm a scaffolder now." With a smile and a chuckle from Tom no more was said, we ate our lunch then back to work. I was really looking forward to learning a new skill.

The scaffolding foreman showed me how to set up the start of the scaffolding around a new block of flats that had the first floor finished so the builders could start on the second floor. As the days and weeks went by I was doing each lift on my own, and all was fine till I got to the eighth floor, it was then I realised I wasn't keen on heights. I was getting very nervous with one foot on the outside scaffold bar and the other foot on the bar going into the building and no safety harness, and nothing between me and God's green earth. I was attempting to put in an upright to start the lift for the ninth floor, when a gust of wind rocked me; I dropped the scaffold bar and fell but just managed to grab the bar I was standing on. The bad language that was shouted at me from the workers below me I can't print but it was very bad, I can tell you! My heart was pounding and I was shaking with fright so I crawled off that scaffolding, I ran down the stairs to the ground floor, I found the little Irish scaffolding foreman and said my favourite saying when I wanted out of a job, "Lick em on – I'm off."

The foreman was very softly spoken and very much a gentleman. He smiled and said "I understand, Dave, you would get used to it in time, I was the same as you when I first started. I don't want you to leave," he said to me. My mind was made up; my nerves were still dancing. "Well if you decide to come back and give it another try you can have your job back," he told me. I thanked him and that was the last time I ever saw him, or did any scaffolding.

That evening I walked into my house and said to my wife, "I've told em to lick em on."

With a painful look on her face my wife replied, "Not again!"

I was very irresponsible in those days (well nothing has changed to this day).

PARKINSON COWEN

Parkinson Cowen were based in the Stechford area of Birmingham, 33, Iron Lane was the entrance to their personnel office. They made gas stoves, or as my mom put it, gas ovens. As I walked in to that office I remember thinking how quiet it was, mind you, nearly all personnel offices were like that and I've walked in to so many it could be in *The Guinness Book of Records*! Any road up I had my interview, all went well and I was told to start the next afternoon as they did a three shift system. I hated shifts as much as I hated being locked up in a factory, mind you, I hated work, I really did hate working, being told what to do so they could make money out of me. I was put on the back end of the ovens where all the panels that had been painted were baked. As they very slowly went along on the conveyer belt, my job was to take them off the conveyer and place them on a trolley that had separate compartments to keep them from getting scratched – they were very hot as you can imagine. When the trolley was full the heat was overbearing; I then pushed them to a cooling down area.

The foreman was Polish and not a very nice man, he was always moaning, nothing suited him. I did one shift on afternoons and one night shift, but on my last night I was so fed up with that foreman I told him to, "Lick em on – I'm off." Well there is a surprise. I worked with the maintenance men in this shop shown when it was being changed around. I was working for Clyde Hopkins.

Showing inside the factory.

Parkinson Cowen factory

POTATO PICKING

My younger brother John and me, we used to go potato picking on the farms around the Warwickshire and Staffordshire counties when we were between jobs, which was nearly all the time. I used to pick him up in my car early in the morning, and travel all around the countryside looking for jobs on the farms. It was usually wet and cold but we loved it, we used to have such laughs. John had a very infectious laugh, and when I was driving and we were telling jokes or saying something that made him laugh, he would start me off – I laughed till I had tears running down my face. So many times I had to stop the car because the tears would blur my vision.

We were very careful when going onto farms as they all had dogs; we were chased many times and John would split his sides laughing at me running to the car terrified. One time we went to a farm in Tamworth, a man named Kingslake owned it, we were led to believe he was the richest man in Tamworth at that time, and was the head of the organisation in that area known as The Round Table, they did a lot of good work for charity. Any road up, we went on to his farm or small holding as it was, and there were piles of hard core so we went to the barn where there was a man working; he gave us the job of levelling out the hard core, and stamping it down. It took a couple of days doing that job; we were paid one pound ten shillings a day and we were very happy with that. I asked, "Have you any other work?"

"Have you ever picked potatoes?" he asked.

"Yes, we both have," I replied, "many times, but we ain't as fast as the ladies," I explained.

"Can you drive a lorry?" he enquired.

"Yes, no problem," I told him.

"Oh good; in the morning you pick up the ladies from here and take them to the field. I will show you where, you follow me."

I did that every morning and it was fun; this potato picking was different from the norm, he had a trailer on the back of the tractor. It was a new machine; we all stood both sides of the trailer, and as the spuds came up on the conveyer belt we had to pick out the spuds which were put on a different belt to a shoot and into a trailer that was running alongside of our trailer, both being pulled by a tractor, it was really much easier than bending down and dragging a sack behind you and picking up the potatoes from the ground – that was back breaking.

We left that farm as the work dwindled and went to another farm that was very short on labour. We started working, picking potatoes at eight a.m., the ladies came at nine a.m. and by ten a.m. they passed us – they made us look like children. The boss asked me to get the tractor and trailer and load up all the bags of potatoes that we and the women had picked; that was a relief, I can tell you, I wasn't any good at picking potatoes, men cannot pick like the women can. When the trailer was loaded with the sacks of spuds, my brother and me took them to the barn and emptied each bag onto a conveyer and they were added to a mountain of spuds already there. After lunch as I was driving the lorry on to the field there was a black bag in the mud, I ran over it, it turned out to be one of the ladies lunch bags with her flask in it, she went barmy, said her husband would beat me up! He didn't, I'm glad to say.

When we went to another farm the next year, it was in the Tamworth area, next to a pub called the Jolly Sailor; I went with my brother in-law, Len. The farmer was John, and he showed us how to clamp up potatoes in the field, the way the Victorians did it. First we dug a trench, lined it with straw then piled up the potatoes in the shape of a tent, then put straw in thick layers all over the potatoes, then we put a tube in the middle of the pile on the top, that was to let the heat out, then we covered it completely with soil, all by hand, a shovel full at a time, that's what is known as clamping up. Those spuds lasted all through the winter, and when they were needed the end of the clamp was opened up, they took out the amount of spuds that were needed, and then closed it up again – the mice loved it, it kept them warm in the cold winter months.

There was a time when John and I worked on different farms because they had a position for only one of us. John worked on a farm that was run by two brothers, I worked across the road on another farm, Blackgreaves Farm it was called. I was driving a tractor and loading

Working in the country side potato picking

the trailer with the sacks of spuds, John was picking spuds. I finished at five thirty, jumped in my car and went to the farm where John was but they were all behind, lots of sacks still in the field waiting to be loaded up on to the trailer. John said, "I can't leave, Dave." So rather than leave him, I offered to load the sacks onto the trailer. By this time it was pouring with rain and I hadn't any rain wear, neither had John, but we worked till seven o'clock. We were like drowned rats and covered in mud – strange thing was we enjoyed it! The farmer gave me ten shillings, so that made me happy, I thought I was doing it for nothing to help my brother out to get him finished and get home. The farmers liked the way I worked so they gave me a job. We both worked there till all the fields had been picked – working on the land gave me much satisfaction. Again cash in hand. All the farms we worked on did more or less the same work, well we did anyway. I enjoyed my brother John's company, and we always worked well together.

RAILWAY

I loved the railway from my very early childhood. The railway goods yard that was in Rupert Street in the Nechells area, that is where I worked for British Rail; I was trained up to drive the three-wheeled scammels known as the Iron Horse. I loved the training; in that yard we had to back the trailers in the tightest of gaps, and I wasn't allowed to touch the sides of anything at all with the trailer. When backing it between two parked trailers, there was only half an inch either side, and you weren't allowed to touch the sides of the other trailers parked there. I practised and practised every day, it seemed it was never going to happen. Then one day it changed, it all fell into place, and then with no effort at all I did it every time. It was the same for all trainees, I've watched them many times, one day they are struggling, then the next day something clicks and it all falls into place.

The next step was taking the cab and trailer (some call the trailer a drag and the cab a unit) on a test. The railway, the L. M. S., that is, had their own examiners, government trained I was told. Onto the road I went. The one thing I was taught when learning to drive a car was never let go of the steering wheel; with an artic you have to do just that, so down the hill I went, and when the examiner shouted "Now!" I hit the foot brake, put on the hand brake and kept one hand on the wheel. "No," he said, "your driving is first class but in order to make sure you don't jack knife, and you didn't that time you kept it straight, I want to see you let go of the steering wheel, hit the foot brake and pull on the trailer brake and the hand brake together, if you don't do it I will fail you." So down the hill I went again. When he shouted, "Now!" I left my hand on the steering wheel. "Right," he said, "yes it was straight, you didn't jack knife. Right, switch off the engine and take a deep breath and relax for one minute. Your driving is excellent, your reversing between the trailers was perfect, in fact it was so good I thought it was a fluke, that's why I got you to do it again, it was just as good the second time but you have to let go of the steering wheel, so I'm going to let you do it again, but I will fail you this time if you don't do as I ask."

So down the hill I went, saying to myself, let the wheel go, let the wheel go, over and over I said it. "Now!" he shouted. I hit all the brakes. "There you go, I knew you could do it," he told me, and made me do it again. I had no trouble at all the third time, and he wrote out my licence there and then.

After he had gone I practised doing it on my own, I did it every time, no problem at all, but to be honest when I had to do it one day for real, I kept my hand on the wheel and I didn't jack-knife. I asked a few drivers and they all said they kept one hand on the wheel. I was so pleased when I passed my test, the one thing I haven't told you is when being trained to drive those three wheelers, it always made one sweat and no one knew why, it just did, it happened to everyone and I was no exception; when backing the trailer up to the deck you had an audience of the drivers that had gone through it themselves, they stood along the wall and laughed, they had it done to them and so did I.

This is exactly how it went, when starting to back the trailer on to the deck the steering wheel would be gripped far too tight, you could see the knuckles going white and the cab would swing from left to right because the steering wheel was moved too much, then the cab would hit the trailer so the wheel was swung in the other direction, which completely ruined the whole exercise and the sweating got worse – being watched of course made it worse. I did my share of laughing at them then, they did it to the raw recruits.

I did most of my driving around the Hockley area of Birmingham. It was tight going around Hockley, that's the jewellery quarter and the parking around there was horrendous. Vehicles parked both sides of the road and down the centre. I worked over every night and did collections from the jewellery quarter to make my wages worth picking up. The sheets that I received from the customers were about a foot square and there was a dozen all joined together, this happened with every collection I did. By the time I did my last collection I had what looked like a mountain of paper; it filled the passenger side of the cab. As we entered the yard just by the entrance, there was a little brick built hut, we gave all the paper work to the man who put it through a copy machine, I then took it to the main yard office but before that I would run into the yard, swing the vehicle round and back it to the deck. I was supposed to put the trailer brake on first but we drivers never did that because there was a slope, only slight but it was enough to stop the trailer from rolling away from the deck. The far end of the deck you couldn't do it as there was no slope to the deck. I didn't know this at first, so I backed up the deck, pulled the trailer release lever which dropped the trailer legs, and as I pulled away all the drivers were laughing – the deck hands had to run after the trailer as it rolled across the yard! I got a good telling off for that; well I never did it again, not at the far end of the deck anyway.

One morning I was told to go to Lawley Street depot, which was a really big railway yard. A young lad about the same age as myself came over to me and said, "Are you from Rupert Street?"

"Yes," I replied.

"Oh good, I've been waiting for you, I want you to deliver house to house with catalogue goods." He told me to back up to a deck where all the parcels were piled high, and lots had fallen into the bay where I was told to back up.

"There are parcels on the floor; I can't back into there," I told him.

"Don't worry," he said, "just run over them." So I did. I could hear the crunching as the parcels got run over. It's no wonder the railways were losing money, I thought to myself. At Rupert Street that never happened, that yard was kept very clean and tidy.

The following day I was sent to Curzon Street railway yard, with twelve rolls of carpet underlay. I roped it up but was too lazy to sheet it, and when I arrived at Curzon Street, to my horror I had lost a roll – I never even noticed it dropping off! I immediately dropped the trailer and run all over the route I had taken. I never found that roll. When I got back to the yard two railway police were waiting for me, and I was questioned for two and three quarter hours – I was being accused of stealing it! It all came to nothing in the end, but I was more careful after that.

So I was put back on delivering empty wooden cases and tea chests all around the jewellery quarter. There was a small firm there that asked me for empty cases with no names on them – I got 3d, three pence, for every case I took to them, and that paid for my breakfast most mornings. The rail company just wanted them gone. At the end of each day I parked my cab in the old stable block right at the bottom of the yard. I worked there almost twelve months! One morning I turned up for work as normal and for reasons I cannot explain I handed in my notice. I was given a form to fill in, on it they asked reason for leaving, but I just didn't know what to say so I put 'fed up' I did miss doing that job for a while but I soon found something different to do.

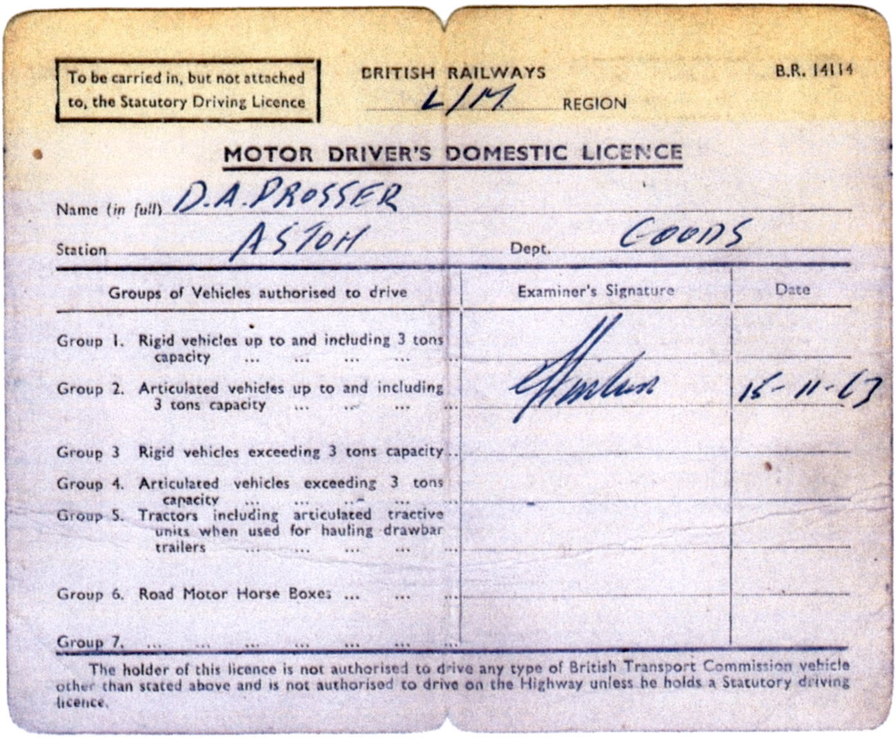

To be carried in, but not attached to, the Statutory Driving Licence

BRITISH RAILWAYS

L/M REGION

B.R. 14114

MOTOR DRIVER'S DOMESTIC LICENCE

Name *(in full)* D.A. PROSSER

Station ASTON Dept. GOODS

Groups of Vehicles authorised to drive	Examiner's Signature	Date
Group 1. Rigid vehicles up to and including 3 tons capacity		
Group 2. Articulated vehicles up to and including 3 tons capacity	[signature]	15-11-63
Group 3 Rigid vehicles exceeding 3 tons capacity...		
Group 4. Articulated vehicles exceeding 3 tons capacity		
Group 5. Tractors including articulated tractive units when used for hauling drawbar trailers		
Group 6. Road Motor Horse Boxes		
Group 7.		

The holder of this licence is not authorised to drive any type of British Transport Commission vehicle other than stated above and is not authorised to drive on the Highway unless he holds a Statutory driving licence.

My licence for driving British Railway vehicles

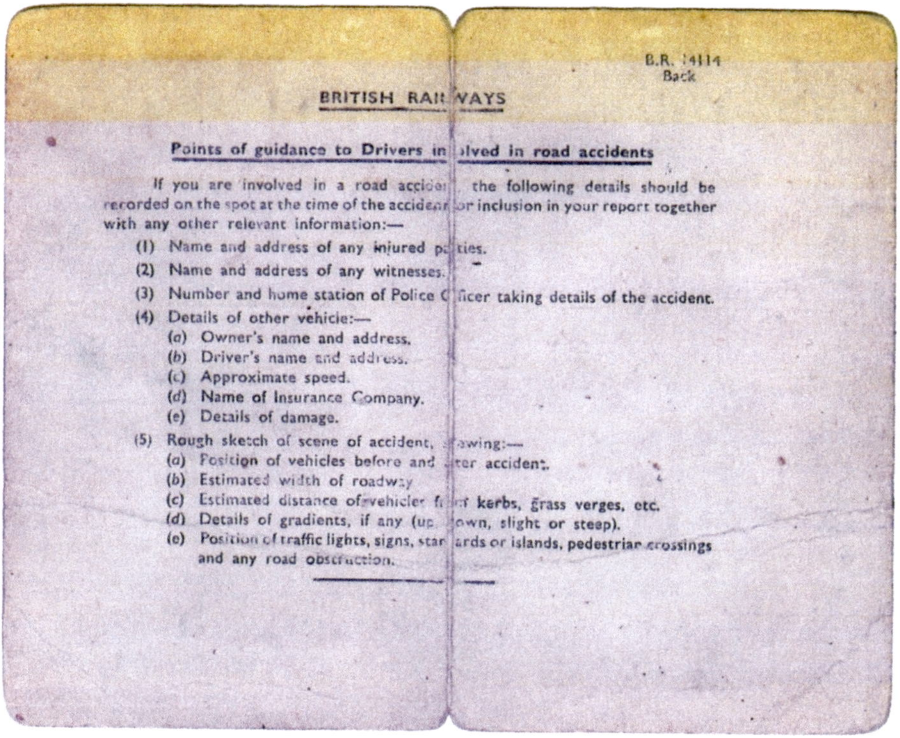

B.R. 14114
Back

BRITISH RAILWAYS

Points of guidance to Drivers involved in road accidents

If you are involved in a road accident, the following details should be recorded on the spot at the time of the accident for inclusion in your report together with any other relevant information:—

(1) Name and address of any injured parties.

(2) Name and address of any witnesses.

(3) Number and home station of Police Officer taking details of the accident.

(4) Details of other vehicle:—
  (*a*) Owner's name and address.
  (*b*) Driver's name and address.
  (*c*) Approximate speed.
  (*d*) Name of Insurance Company.
  (*e*) Details of damage.

(5) Rough sketch of scene of accident, showing:—
  (*a*) Position of vehicles before and after accident.
  (*b*) Estimated width of roadway
  (*c*) Estimated distance of vehicles from kerbs, grass verges, etc.
  (*d*) Details of gradients, if any (up, down, slight or steep).
  (*e*) Position of traffic lights, signs, standards or islands, pedestrian crossings and any road obstruction.

My licence for driving British Railway vehicles

I drove these three wheeled Scammels in 1963

ALBERT HALL

After leaving the railway I went to a builder's type yard. The builder contracted to the council doing pavement and curb stone laying. The owner had three tipper lorries and five gangs doing the laying of the pavements – tarmacing mostly, they were doing away with paving slabs at that time. Any road up, this firm was in Cooks Lane, Tile Cross. The builder asked me where I had been working and what I had driven. "A three-wheeled railway scammel."

He looked a little shocked. "So have you ever driven a tipper, young man?"

"No, but they must be easier to drive than an artic lorry," I replied. "If it's got wheels, I can drive it."

He looked at me funny. "OK, there is the lorry, go to Kellymead Road. There is a gang tarmacing, go and shovel up all the rubbish they have created onto the lorry and come back here with it."

So I did as I was asked. I pulled into the yard a couple of hours later. "You managed that all right then. OK, take it to the rubbish tip in Meriden." He gave me the directions; I did that, and got back to the yard. "Good," he said, "you can have the job; start tomorrow."

The next morning the JCB loaded the lorry to capacity with broken slabs. I was given the address, it was a private house. I remember that day well only for the reason it was a very cold day. The boss sat in a shed that was his office, opposite the door which was wide open, and all he wore was a vest – everyone else had donkey jackets on and gloves. The area I was given to take the load of slabs to was Sheldon, near the Birmingham airport. I knocked on the door. "Good morning, sir," I said to the man of the house in a cheerful voice and shivering at the same time. "Broken slabs."

"Great; tip them on the garden for me please."

"No problem, sir."

So I did as he had asked. When he saw the amount, he had a fit. "I only ordered five tons!" I'd tipped about twenty tons. "What the hell am I going to do with all this?" he asked, rubbing his head with both hands.

"Sell it to your neighbours," I told him.

"Ah, that's a good idea, I will do just that," he said.

Some weeks later I went down that road and it seemed nearly every garden had broken slabs in them. Not much different went on there, every day the same, delivering slabs and curb stones to the gangs and shovelling rubbish on to the lorry and tipping it at the tip. Guess what? Yes, three and a half months later I handed in my notice.

BOOTHS

Booths are an aluminium company in the Kitts Green area of Birmingham, making tin foil for wrapping food up and also making many other items from aluminium.

I went into the office and asked as I usually did, "Have you any vacancies?" To my surprise they said, "Yes, we are looking for an overhead crane driver."

"I've never done that before," I told the personnel officer.

"That's OK," he replied, "we will train you." Great, I thought, another string to my bow. "Do you mind having a medical now?" he asked me.

"What, right now?" I asked.

"Yes, we have our own surgery, and a doctor."

So off I went to a very clean surgery. All was well until I was told, "You need glasses, son." I was shocked and disappointed. I had never been in an overhead crane, I've driven cranes, I've used overhead cranes, looking up at it with a hand control, but I've never sat in one. I'm retired now and I've no wish to sit in one. Any road up, I got my glasses and went back to Booths with them. I was told they didn't need an overhead crane driver any longer as that vacancy had been filled, so they offered me a job running a machine. It was a rolling machine, rolling out square blocks of aluminium; these were about three feet square and a foot thick. It rolled it backwards and forwards till it became tin foil. It was a very clean work shop. When I was interviewed for the job by the foreman he asked me, "Now are you sure there isn't a better job out there that you would prefer to do, before I set you on?"

I told him there wasn't. It was a three shift system; I started on mornings, then one week afternoons, then the night shift for five nights. It was summer and I longed for the great outdoors, not to be locked in a horrible factory, so on the last night shift being a Friday, I handed in my notice. The foreman wasn't very happy with me, he said, "I asked you if there was a better job out there, didn't I?"

I got my wages and started a new job on the Monday, delivering bread door to door for the Co-op bakery. Their bakery was in Stechford, the same bakery I had worked at as a boy and as a rounds man; it's a wonder they took me back. I wasn't there long; as usual I got bored and left after a few months.

CARS

After leaving the Co-op bakery I signed on the dole. I hung around the garage where my two eldest brothers had started up their own business doing car repairs in Orphanage Road, Erdington, Birmingham. It was a very large wooden building with enough space to house, or should I say park, four cars. I was just sixteen at the time, so I watched and tried to learn as much as I could for when the day came that I would own a car. I picked up a few tips. I passed my test when I was twenty, by that time my brother Donald had bought a shop in Booth Street, Handsworth, and altered the back yard into a car repair work shop. They sprayed cars, did de-cokes on car engines, and under-sealed cars. They dug a pit – it was a good work shop.

They had converted the shop premises into flats; I had a downstairs flat there after I got married. I used to help fetching spares for the cars that were being fitted with new parts, and I did a little spraying. Sometimes I did a few de-cokes and regrinding in the valves. I was taught a lot by my eldest brother Donald, in fact it was him that taught me to drive. I passed my test after my ninth lesson – twelve hours of driving then I passed my test! Donald taught many to drive. When I passed my test my brother sold me a ten hundred weight van for fifty pounds, of which I paid twenty five pounds back and that took nearly six months to pay that, so he let me off with the rest of the payments because I was always helping him. I travelled all over England in that van; it had windows put in the sides and two seats in the back. It started to burn oil so I took out all the necessary bolts, stood on the wings, and with a rope round the engine and around my neck I lifted that engine out, rested it on the wing, with my wife steadying it till I got off the van, then I put my arms around the engine lifted it off the van and placed it on the ground. No way could I have done that with today's engines. I remembered what my brother had taught me, so I striped the engine down, put in new rings and new big end shells, (those are on the ends of the pistons) that's what most people did that were not well off – poor is a better word.

My car driving licence, 1963

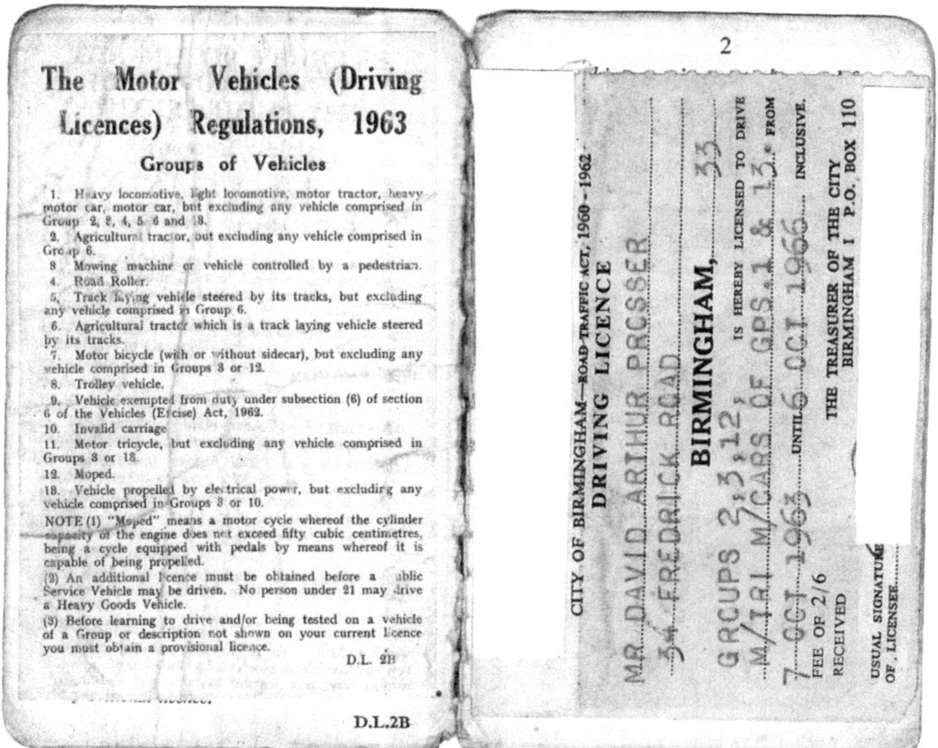

The Motor Vehicles (Driving Licences) Regulations, 1963

Groups of Vehicles

1. Heavy locomotive, light locomotive, motor tractor, heavy motor car, motor car, but excluding any vehicle comprised in Group 2, 2, 4, 5, 6 and 13.
2. Agricultural tractor, but excluding any vehicle comprised in Group 6.
3. Mowing machine or vehicle controlled by a pedestrian.
4. Road Roller.
5. Track laying vehicle steered by its tracks, but excluding any vehicle comprised in Group 6.
6. Agricultural tractor which is a track laying vehicle steered by its tracks.
7. Motor bicycle (with or without sidecar), but excluding any vehicle comprised in Groups 3 or 12.
8. Trolley vehicle.
9. Vehicle exempted from duty under subsection (6) of section 6 of the Vehicles (Excise) Act, 1962.
10. Invalid carriage
11. Motor tricycle, but excluding any vehicle comprised in Groups 3 or 13.
12. Moped.
13. Vehicle propelled by electrical power, but excluding any vehicle comprised in Groups 3 or 10.

NOTE (1) "Moped" means a motor cycle whereof the cylinder capacity of the engine does not exceed fifty cubic centimetres, being a cycle equipped with pedals by means whereof it is capable of being propelled.
(2) An additional licence must be obtained before a Public Service Vehicle may be driven. No person under 21 may drive a Heavy Goods Vehicle.
(3) Before learning to drive and/or being tested on a vehicle of a Group or description not shown on your current licence you must obtain a provisional licence.

D.L. 2B

D.L.2B

2

CITY OF BIRMINGHAM—ROAD TRAFFIC ACT, 1960-1962
DRIVING LICENCE
MR DAVID ARTHUR PROSSER
34 FREDRICK ROAD
BIRMINGHAM, 33
GROUPS 2,3,12, IS HEREBY LICENSED TO DRIVE
M/TRI M/CARS OF GPS. 1 & 13. FROM
7 OCT 1963 UNTIL 6 OCT 1966 INCLUSIVE.
FEE OF 2/6 RECEIVED
THE TREASURER OF THE CITY
BIRMINGHAM 1 P.O. BOX 110
USUAL SIGNATURE OF LICENSEE

My car driving licence, 1963

CLYDE HOPKINS

This firm was situated just down the road from where I lived at that time in the Stechford area, just across the road from the Atlas cinema, where I used to stand outside with my friend Trevor asking the people if they would take us in to the cinema. They had an office next to the snooker hall where me and my other friend Johnny used to waste a few hours every Friday after knocking off for the weekend from Cooks the clock face makers.

Clyde Hopkins was a maintenance firm; I did all sorts of jobs for this firm and worked for them on and off a few times. This one time they gave me a job on nights at the Lucas factory in Great Kings street in the Hockley area, and I was assigned to the maintenance department. I worked with a Scotsman, who was working making all sorts of things out of sheet metal. He was a very soft spoken man who would only make things that were perfect, he was a perfectionist and very skilled. I learned a lot from him; he taught me how to make a tool box to put my spanners in, in fact I made two, one for me and one for my brother Donald, I also made a pair of car stands for Donald.

There were six men that worked in that department; they all got their heads down at midnight on makeshift beds in the office – the daytime foreman's office. All those men had worked on nights for years; one had done thirty five years, the youngest had done nineteen. Anyway, one night after midnight when I was quietly making one of the tool boxes, I was told I was being too noisy and had to get my head down come midnight or he would get me sacked. So I was sent to bed, ha, ha – it's true, I was. It would have been easy for him to do that as well, as I didn't work for Lucas's direct, I was supplied labour, it was an easy way of earning a living, it's no wonder firms went broke. Why I was there I had no idea, I did nothing for Lucas's that would have made the slightest of difference me being there or not, all I did was to make things out of metal for myself. Mind you, I was useful once, yes, only once. The maintenance man from the main factory who had nothing to do with this side of the firm needed a hand to fix a conveyer belt that had broken in the main building. So I was woken up at one thirty (yes, one thirty, what a nerve, eh?), it was an overhead conveyer, so I was close to the ceiling, it was hot and I sweated like a pig, (do pigs sweat?) it was so uncomfortable – it was very high up. I was taking out bolts by the dozens, it was steel rollers with a rubber belt running over them and the belt had broken. It was repaired then put back; it was harder putting it back trying to line up all the holes to re-bolt it all back together.

After working there I was transferred to a steel mill in the Black Country. I can't remember the name of it, but what I do remember is it was like going back once again to the Dickensian times – braziers glowing with red hot coke, and the fumes from coke was awful; it brought back the memories of my childhood when my mom burnt coke because it was cheaper than coal. The taste in one's mouth was awful (did you like that, *one's* mouth, that's not me talking – in my gob I would have said as a youngster). There were boxes surrounding each of the braziers for the men to sit on for their breaks. The factory was cladded in corrugated tin panels, there were more holes in the roof and the walls than in the braziers, and it was plain to see why they had braziers all around the factory floor.

I worked nights at that factory, and I was given the job of looking after a machine that looked like it could have been used in the *Doctor Who* films. I have no idea what the machine did or was used for, all I know is every now and then it would throw out a blue green crystal; there were long plastic pipes all around the top of the machine and they came down the outside of it and attached in the middle of the machine. It was round, about ten foot high and the round plastic tubes were about two inches across. Air went through them and every now and again a tube would come off at the top of the machine and made a loud hissing noise, so I had to push it back on. When there was a small pile of crystals I shovelled them into a wheel barrow, took them outside and shovelled them onto a mountain of crystals – what they did with them I have no idea.

There was a similar machine next to the one that I was looking after, and it was attended to by an elderly man, well he looked old to me, I suppose he was worn out by that time, working in those conditions. About four feet away from those two machines was a brazier with an armchair – that was the old fella's – a couple of boxes and a bench. I asked the old fella if I could use the bench. "That's OK," he said. "The armchair is mine." So I pushed on a tube that had come off, shovelled the few crystals that were there and threw them on the outside pile. It was now twelve midnight.

I said to the old fella, "I'm getting my head down for an hour, OK?," He pulled a face, and shrugged his shoulders, so I rolled up my coat, put it under my head for a pillow, lay on that bench and fell asleep.

I woke up with a start, it was a quarter to six in the morning and I knocked off at six. All the tubes were off the machine hissing like mad and there was a very large pile of crystals around the machine. I pushed all the tubes back on, and it took three barrow loads of crystals to clear the machine, it was now just after six. I was putting on my coat when the day shift man who looked after the machine came in. "Was everything OK with the machine through the night?" he asked me.

"Yeah, no problems," I told him.

"That makes a change," he replied. I never went back there again so I have no idea if that machine with its pipes off all night did any damage to whatever it was making. The next afternoon I phoned up the office and handed in my notice, telling them I didn't like working nights – me work; now there is a laugh for you.

A WORKSHOP IN HANDSWORTH

My brother Donald asked me to help him for a short while in his new car repair shop; he was in partnership with some of his work mates at that time, they all worked at Fisher and Ludlow's, later to be renamed B.M.C. Apart from making the tea, running errands and fetching paint to spray the cars with, Donald taught me how to strip an engine and do a de-coke. We had fish and chips every Saturday dinnertime.

I even towed cars in from wherever they broke down, but well before that Donald was teaching me how to drive. He was a very good instructor. I had nine lessons; seven were for two hundred yards up the road to the pub, the Lea Village Tavern. It was on that car park where it all clicked into place. He went inside the pub to get a pint, and as I sat in the van, I thought to myself, if I let the clutch out slowly, when I start to move, if I dip it I will stop. So I started to drive backwards and forwards. That's easy, I thought. Donald's brother in-law, Gordon, was sitting on the wall watching me. As Donald came out with Gordon's pint in his hand, Gordon said, "It's just clicked, Don."

"About time," he replied.

So seven lessons, then the other two were four hours long. One day he asked me how many lessons I'd had.

"Don't know," I replied.

"It's seven. I know this Dave because every time you back off my driveway you take a paling off the gate." So I counted them and sure enough there were seven palings on the floor behind the gate. As we went down the road, I told him he didn't need to shout. "Is that so?" he said. "OK I won't shout anymore. So he quietly said, "Stop here." I carried on. "OK," he said, "stop by that tree." I still went past the tree, so he screamed, "Stop!" I hit the brakes and stopped dead. "There you are, see, I asked you to stop twice and you didn't; when I shouted stop, you did. You are stubborn, Dave, that's why I shout at you – you only obey my instructions when I shout. So now I want you to change up and down the box from this corner to that one and see how many times you can do it."

Well I got to third gear when I reached the corner. "You can only do one up the box before you reach the corner," I told him, so he got in the driver's seat. He went up and down that box a lot of times.

"Now believe what I tell you." so I did. I failed my first test, but I passed on the second one, so all in all I had eleven driving lessons, that's counting the two tests. Since then I passed a test for my H.G.V. Class Two, and advanced driving tests for the army to carry chemicals, poisons and hazardous materials. I've also drove a coach, troop carrier, a crane and many other different small vehicles. Driving changed the way I could earn a living. Variety, yes, I had that, when in between jobs I helped my brother in his garage. Thinking about it, I was always between jobs.

PONDSFORDS

Pondsfords was a maintenance firm based in Handsworth, Birmingham. They contracted out their labour force to any firm that needed any and all types of machinery moving or transporting anywhere in the country. They did all kinds of steel erections for machinery to stand on, and staging as well. My job was a fitter's mate, known now as a semi skilled engineer. I travelled all round the country; I liked the freedom of this job.

One firm I remember well was Pirelli Tyres, it was very noisy. There was a young girl in a very long room with machines that looked to me like very large sewing machines. The room was spotlessly clean. There were lots of those machines in rows and that young lady looked after them on her own, and all day long she sang at the top off her voice. She always seemed very happy.

After that I went to many different factories, I even went to a power station called Hams Hall. Why we went there I have no idea; we did ten minutes of welding on the first day, the rest of the week we did nothing. What confused me was they had their own maintenance work force that did all the welding themselves. They weren't very nice to us I remember; I don't think they wanted us there. When we walked in on the morning and said, "Good morning," we never got a reply. Were they trying to tell us something? Yes, I think they were.

As per usual I got fed up, handed in my notice, and got a job at Factory Plant Removals doing the same type of work, but as a driver as well. This firm was also in the Handsworth area of Birmingham at that time.

FACTORY PLANT REMOVALS

I lived at number 78, Downing Street, Handsworth in Birmingham. The rent was fifteen shillings a week but it went down to fourteen shillings and ten pence when the area changed to Smethwick. The house was directly on to the pavement. All the houses at the back which would have been up the entry into a yard had been demolished, and my house had a demolition order on it. I got a job just around the corner in Brearly Street, with a firm known as Factory Plant Removals. They moved heavy machinery anywhere in the country to whatever factory or site they were asked to move it to or from; they worked out of town quite a lot.

Not long after I started work there I was sent to Blackpool for a week. We took heavy machines to a factory there and bolted them in place. I cannot for the life of me remember the name of that factory, but I enjoyed the experience, it was the first time I had bolted down a machine. The machines were something to do with glass fibre, as the firm made car bodies in glass fibre – they would be wouldn't they? I do say daft things at times, ha, ha. It was in the middle of winter, it was raining all the time I was there, and the winds were so strong it was hard to walk; very tiring.

After the first week the boss asked me if I would go back with him, as he needed a driver for another job. I drove back in a Commer van, I had to work the wipers by hand because the electric motor had burnt out, and the steering was all over the place. I drove one-handed all the way back from Blackpool to West Bromwich, then off the M6 to the yard in Handsworth. I would get locked up these days for driving such a bad unroadworthy vehicle – that van should have been driven to the scrap yard.

When I arrived back at the yard I picked up a Guy lorry, it was a seven man crew cab, it had a big jib on the back of it, and the wheels were as tall as me, the same type as Pickfords used at that time. I hooked up a low loader trailer and went to Salters factory in West Bromwich, they were moving to new premises, I think it was in Willenhall; anyway it was in the Black Country. I had to stand up to drive that vehicle; if I sat down I could only just about see over the steering wheel.

I worked all the weekend at that Salters factory getting those machines out, we used metal tubes as rollers. As the machine went forward I would take the back roller and put it in the front of the machine. It worked well till we hit uneven ground, then with six feet long solid steel crow bars we bared the machine along till it came in contact with the rollers again. I really enjoyed the physical side of that job, it kept me fit and strong and sometimes knackered, fit for nothing; that type of employment was defiantly no good for weaklings. When we got those machines outside we put chains around them, hooked them up to the crane, or jib as we called it, which was on the back of the wagon, then slowly moved to the trailer and loaded it on to the trailer. Those trailers are known as low loaders. We got four machines on at a time, with heavy duty chains they were safely held in place, all seven men got into the cab and I drove it to Salters new factory. As I had passed my test on those railway three-wheel Scammels I was ok reversing, mind you low loaders are a different ball game as the saying goes. Well I backed it into the yard perfectly, but on the second load I made a complete mess of it, I just couldn't do it, so I asked the other driver if he would back it in. "No problem, Dave." He never took the mick, he just did it for me; he was a nice man to work with.

On the Sunday there were no buses running to West Bromwich, so I had to use my car, well in those days that area was a ghost town on a Sunday, no cars running, nothing. I hadn't any road tax on my car, but I thought it, will be all right; I will hide it round the side road behind the foreman's car. I had only been working for twenty minutes when the foreman shouted, "Dave, there's a copper wants a word." I explained my predicament to the officer but he would have none of it – he only looked about fourteen,

I asked him how long he had been an officer. Two days on the beat, it's no wonder he wouldn't let me off, he was earning his brownie points. I got a fine of twenty five pounds; all that hard work I did went to paying that fine. I was allowed to pay a pound a week, which was a lot out of my wages every week, I mean, my rent then was only fourteen shillings and ten pence a week, so it hurt to pay a pound for my fine. I know I should have taxed my car; I was saving up for it, that's why I was working all the hours God sent, as the saying goes.

The next job we went to was in the Aldridge area, at a factory called Crabtree, they were doing the new tableware called Melamine, I was told it was a new material on the market at that time. We did to be honest borrow one or two items of that new tableware to take home. We were installing a brand new lathe into their redesigned work shop, I wasn't the driver that day, an Irishman named Billy was. He picked up the lathe off the trailer and I asked him if he was going to put the hydraulic legs down and put the skates under them, as those skates allowed the cab to move forward away from the trailer. "It will be OK," he replied, "it's not that heavy." As he moved away from the trailer, the weight of the lathe tipped up the cab; it hit the ground hard and broke some of the casting off one corner of the lathe. Billy had to let the cables from the crane down to lower the cab to the ground. A little red-faced he said, "I didn't think it was that heavy." The boss blew a gasket, well both bosses, theirs and ours. Billy nearly lost his job; he was one of those people that thought he knew it all. Then to make matters worse the machine wouldn't go through the door so I took the door off, I had done that so many times on other jobs, it was the norm, and we did what was needed to do to get the job done. We had the machine halfway through the door; it was going through just right with the door off, when we noticed all the workers at the factory were in the yard. We all thought there must be a fire or it was a fire drill, when a loud mouthed man came up to us and demanded to know who had taken the door off. "I did," I told him, "but I will put it back on as soon as the machine is clear of the door." He had called a strike because of little old me.

"I want you all off the premises," he was saying in a very loud voice.

"Why?" I asked.

"Why? Why?" he bellowed. "We have a carpenter and that's his job. You are not a qualified carpenter are you?"

"No, but we always do things like take out windows and remove doors." I was apologizing, almost kissing his feet.

"People like you can put skilled men out of work!" He went on and on. The management was trying to calm him down, he really did go over the top; talk about power mad, he kept insisting he wanted us off the premises. It took one and a half hours to get him to understand we put that machine in place but we never bolted it down, we were told to leave it. The boss told me some time later that the company claimed off my boss's insurance, and they got a brand new machine. We didn't fit it; I assume they got another contractor to fit their new machine as we never went back there, nor was I allowed to put that door back on.

The next Monday we went to the Aston University to erect a very big ariel mast on the top of it. We had to winch up four twenty feet long tubes, the circumference must have been something like eighteen inches, one at a time. With two cables bolted to the anchor points used by the window cleaners, we used two winches with long handles on them. By pushing the handle backwards and forwards the cable went though the winches one inch at a time. There were four of us, three Irishmen and this little old Brummie, me, we took it in turns to winch up those tubes, it was quite tiring. When at the top, we man handled them to the other side of the roof, and as we got the second one to the roof top, the tall fella shouted as he tried to lift it on his own, "Come on you idiots, this is heavy!"

Little Billy put his hand around the throat of the tall fella till he almost passed out. He was a violent man, little or nothing or anyone scared him, and the tall fella was his mate. He said, "Don't you ever shout like that again or call me an idiot." The tall fella never said a word. I just can't remember his name, the tall fella that is. It took a few minutes for Billy to calm down.

When it was dinnertime we went down in the lift as there were no stairs. I sat in my car to eat my lunch, and just before dinner break was over the boss turned up. "You got two tubes up I see; well done."

"I reckon we could pull those two up together," I said to him, "that would save us time."

Me and my big mouth – when the others came back the boss said, “You carry on up, and I will sling the tubes.”

As we were winching up the tubes the tall man said, “This is bloody hard, I bet Norman has put both tubes on, he thinks we are donkeys.” (Norman was the boss’s name.) All three of them were getting very angry.

We finally got them to the top, and I said, “Well at least we can go home early, it wasn’t that bad,” hoping they would think, that’s true, we can knock off early. I was hoping the boss wouldn’t come to see us but he did. As he got out of the lift they ran up to him and started shouting abuse at him. “What the hell do you think we are, donkeys? Why did you put the two tubes on, don’t you think we work hard enough?” I could see the boss was getting worried even a little frightened, and by this time I felt very nervous.

The boss said, “Someone told me to.” I stood behind the big fella hoping the boss wouldn’t see me. “He told me to,” he said pointing to me. As they turned to have a go at me, the boss ran to the lift and disappeared, so there I was stuck on the highest roof of the university, no lift because the boss had taken it, and no other way down! The three Irishmen knew how to get me off that roof, but I couldn’t fly! I was now very nervous but I thought, I mustn’t show it, the three Irishmen were out for blood, mine to be exact. The one man known as Pat had only been in England a week or so. I’m not sure, but I don’t think he could read or write, but his farming skills were first class the other two told me.

Pat said pointing to me, “He is going over the edge.” They were all so angry I couldn’t talk to them as they approached me.

“You’re going over,” the tall one said, so I ran to the edge of the building, I was dying inside – there is a time in life when a man has to stand and be counted, that time had come for me.

I stood on the edge of that building and said in a calm voice, “I have a grip like iron and I guarantee two of you will go over with me.”

They stopped dead in their tracks and the toughest one of them all said, “He ain’t worth it, come on lets go down.”

I was so scared I nearly wet myself. What do I do now? There is only one lift and no stairs. Oh well, I thought, if I get a good beating up in the lift that will be better than going over the edge. As I approached the lift, I said, "Sorry lads, at least we go home early."

I was shaking inside. As we entered the lift Pat, the man that had only been in this country a week, took the fire extinguisher off the wall of the lift and was hitting the top of it pointing at me. When Billy asked him what he was doing, he replied, "I'm going to spray him with it," meaning me of course.

"Put it back," Billy told him, "leave him alone." He had calmed down by this time. "He is right, we have finished early." But he wouldn't listen; he just kept on hitting the top hoping it would work; what he didn't know (thank God) was he had to take off the cap, and then strike the plunger on the top. It felt like a lifetime waiting for that lift to stop! As the doors opened I shot out of that lift so fast my shoes melted, well you know what I mean! I got into my car, my heart was pounding, I was shaking, and that's as close to death as I ever want to be.

The next morning I went to see the boss in his office – I had a real go at him. "You can sack me if you like; you nearly got me killed yesterday! Why did you tell them it was me? You could have said you couldn't remember?"

"I know, Dave," he said, "I'm sorry but they scared me so I left thinking the situation might calm down without me around."

"Well I ain't working with them again," I told him.

"OK, Dave, you can drive for the other gang." Great, I thought, all Brummies.

One morning a couple of weeks later, I walked into the yard and there stood a man all six feet three of him, looking like he had never had a wash. He was unshaven and he wore the oldest overcoat I had ever seen. He looked poorer than me. He was as broad as he was tall – a real tough looking character. I smoked in those days, I had three cigarettes to last me all day. I lit one up. "Give me a ciggy," he said in an angry voice.

"I've only got two to last me all day," I told him.

He took his hands out of his pockets. "I said, give me a ciggy." He scared me to death so I gave him one. Here we go again, I thought, I'm going to hand in my notice. Those types of firms always employed

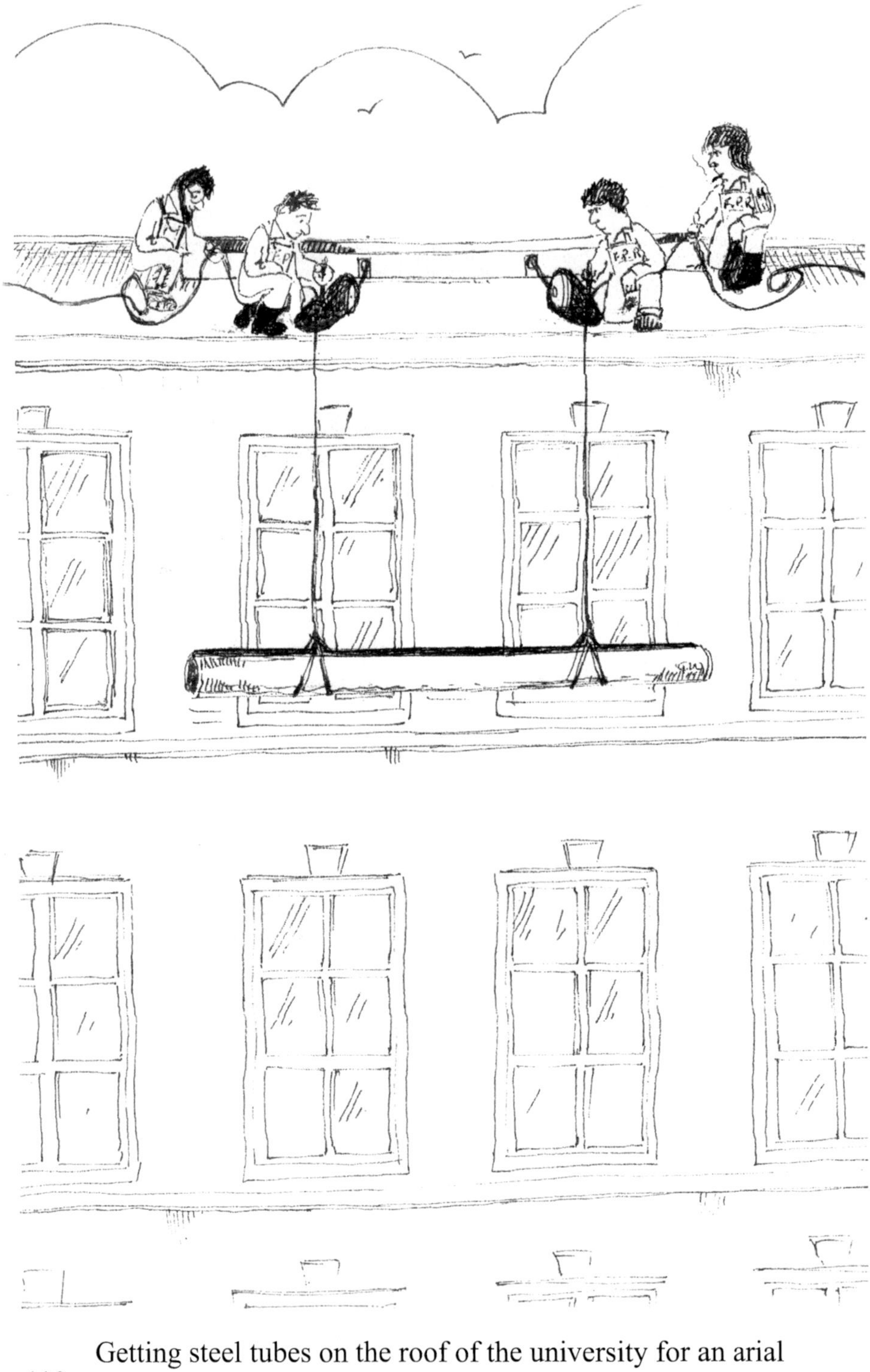

Getting steel tubes on the roof of the university for an arial those types of men. When I got home I was thinking, I will hand in my notice in the morning.

The next morning I went to see the boss and said I was thinking of handing in my notice. That same morning that angry man wasn't around. Good, I hope he has packed up, I was thinking.

On that evening I parked up my wagon and the boss called me and said, "That rough looking fella that made you give him a fag, he has been done for murder. When he got home last night his wife was in her friend's house and he wanted his tea, so he knocked on the friend's door, the man of the house came out and said, "She ain't coming out, I'm keeping her here." So the angry man went home, got a big knife and went back to the friend's house. He knocked on the door, and when the fella opened it, the angry man stabbed him to death."

"I've had it here boss. Lick em on – I'm off," and off I went. That's one firm I never missed working for.

WELLMAN INCANDESCENT

Wellman Incandescent was a good firm to work for, based in Cornwall Street in the Handsworth area of Birmingham. When I went for my interview I was asked, "What type of work are you looking for?"

"Anything," I replied, "I can do many things."

"Can you drive a crane or have you had anything to do with cranes? We are looking for a mobile crane driver," the personnel officer said in a doubtful tone.

"No problem," I replied. "If it's got wheels I can do it." I'd learned that by being confident it gave a good impression, so long as you didn't come across cocky or cheeky.

"What did you say?" he asked.

"If it's got wheels I can drive it."

He laughed. "Well for your cheek, come with me." We walked to the bottom of the yard, and he pointed to the oldest crane I have ever seen – it was just steel girders with a jib on the top, a cast iron seat, three wheels, two at the front and one in the centre at the rear, and solid rubber tyres. Boy it was old. Smiling, he asked, "Well, what do you think? He could see the shocked look on my face.

"Yes," I replied, "no problem."

"OK, start tomorrow and bring your P-45 with you and your insurance cards." On the card were stamps. The firm you worked for had to put a stamp on the card, one every week for the whole year, these were for insurance covering you if you were off sick from work and towards your pension when you retire. (Sick notes from the doctor were charged at a shilling in those days.)

I started next morning, another string to my bow of life, I thought. Well, I had a shock coming. I drove into one of the workshops, they made lampposts at this firm, and the shock I had when I put my foot on the brake and nothing happened! I gripped the steering wheel and pressed down with my foot with every ounce of strength I could muster. I just managed to stop in time as I was about to go through the

Putting tubes in works shop to be turned into lampposts.

back wall which was corrugated iron sheets. What have I let myself in for, I thought to myself. The yard foreman laughed and said, "Now you know why the last driver left."

Without road tax I used to take it on the road about once every fortnight. The steering was all over the place – the steering wheel shook from left to right, it was all I could do to keep it something like straight; the engine sounded like a load of nuts and bolts going round in a tin drum, and when it rained I got wet, no cab, no cover whatsoever.

I lived just around the corner from the firm so I went home to dinner. My wife asked me how I got on. She couldn't believe that such vehicles were still being used, actually neither could I. When I first started to drive it, because the brakes were so inefficient I used to slam it in reverse, this was the most efficient way of stopping it. Trouble was, by doing it that way, eventually it stripped the gears. Whenever I wanted to get out of working I did that reverse stunt and it went into the workshop for three days at a time. The maintenance men used to go mad and the language they shouted at me would make your hair curl; I was threatened with annihilation more times than I could shake a stick at.

There was another crane, a modern iron fairy – the driver sat in that crane in his heated cab reading a book. He moved to do a lift about twice, and then it was for only ten minutes. Some days, he didn't move at all, and there was me not a moment to myself most days. Still, he had worked there forever so he had earned that cushy job. One thing I'm sure of, that crane I drove belonged in a museum. Well at least when having conversations with the older seniors about work, I can say if they talk about cranes, I've been there, done that. Yes, it was another string to my bow of life, even though I only did it for three months. Only three months, I hear you say, well that was normally all I could do any job for.

As I was walking home one dinnertime, an elderly gentleman asked me, "Have you been working at Wellman's long?"

"No," I replied, "only a couple of months."

"Do you like it?" he asked.

"It's OK," I replied. "To be honest, I don't like work," I told him.

"I've worked at Wellman's since I was thirteen, I don't know anything else. Don't you make that mistake, do as many things as you can, son, variety is the spice of life." I had already had lots of different jobs, so I was having my variety. Then to my surprise he said, "I suppose you are going home to get your leg over."

"I hope so," I replied, knowing full well I wouldn't.

"Yes," he said, "I can remember when I was like you, son, I used to rush home, I just couldn't wait to get her knickers off." Then with a laugh he said, "I could sit and watch her knit a pair now." That's one conversation I will never forget.

CO-OP BAKERY HANDSWORTH

After leaving Wellman Incandescent I got a job at the Co-op bakery in Handsworth, I doubled up with a rounds man who had worked there from a boy; that's what they used to do, start you on as a boy, then when you became eighteen they trained you up to become a rounds man, then you had to learn how to order the bread and cakes, calculate if the money was correct, then once you got all the items required, how to fill in the rounds book at every call. It seemed hard at first but like everything in life, when you got used to it you could do it blindfold as the saying goes. When the rounds man gave the bosses the OK, if there was a round going it was offered to you, if no round was available they made you work on the deck. I liked that job working on the deck, or if a rounds boy had a day off they doubled you up on that round.

One Monday morning I was asked to do a round as the rounds man was off sick. They gave me a boy that was lazier than me, he was useless. I told him, "Under no circumstances do you drive the van."

"It's only electric," he replied, "I can drive these, they are easy."

"Well, easy or not, you do not drive this electric van," I repeated. Those vans had two very large batteries underneath, one each side of the van almost the length of it. I was delivering all around the Ladywood area of Birmingham, and nineteen per cent of that round was flats. I was delivering to one block of flats, and as I got to the third floor, I looked over the balcony just in time to see the lad getting into the van to drive it. I shouted to him very loudly not to drive it, but he pretended not to hear me. Next to the block of flats was a row of terraced houses, the type with no front gardens. The front door opened onto the pavement, just like the house I lived in at that time, and I watched in horror as he drove up the hill. Suddenly he turned left, mounted the pavement and drove straight into the front door of the house, smashing it open. I ran to him in case he was hurt, but when I saw he was OK I gave him a telling off he will never in his life forget. He was shaking. The front of the van was smashed but I was still able to finish the round. I phoned the bosses who arranged to get the door of the house replaced. The lad kept saying, "Please don't get me the sack; say you did it."

"No way," I told him, "I have a family to support; I'm not getting the sack for your stupidity."

When the bosses asked me if he was any good, I said, "He will be an asset to the company in the future." I was lying, he was useless.

Any road up, almost at the end of that round I knocked on the door of a customer, and a very pretty lady opened the door. "Good afternoon, madam, would you like any nice cakes or biscuits, I have a good selection on the van today?" (I got commission on the confectionery.)

"You must be joking," she said to me, "I've got seven kids."

I laughed. "You haven't, you ain't old enough to have seven kids." (I really thought she wasn't.)

"Oh what a lovely thing to say; you can take me to bed tomorrow, I will show you what real sex is," she told me. I went as red as a beetroot. She laughed at my red face. "I will look out for you tomorrow. What time will you be here?" she asked me.

"About this time," I replied.

She gave a shudder and said, "I will look forward to it."

Well I wasn't sure if I was excited or scared to death. So back at the yard the van went into the work shop. When I got home I told the wife about my day, had my tea, and settled down to watch the television.

A couple of days later I was put on a round in the Kingstanding area, that rounds man was on holiday. It turned out he was the shop steward for the rounds men. The rounds boy was very well dressed and nicely spoken; he was also very cocky and very cheeky. How it worked on a round was like this: he had a little book and he served half the customers; he wrote down what each customer had that day, and on a Friday and a Saturday he delivered to all the customers, while I collected the money. The way I worked was that at the end of every third road I would ask the lad who was my rounds boy, to tell me what each of his customers had, and I entered it into my book. So at the end of the third road I asked him to tell me what his customers had had. He replied, "I'm not telling you and you can't make me."

"it's my money you are playing with here," I told him.

He laughed, "Your money? It's the Co-op's money, not yours."

"If I'm short, it comes out of my wages. If I lose money on this round I will make sure it comes out of your wages, not mine."

"My rounds man is the shop steward, I know what I can do and can't do."

"I'm your rounds man now, and you will do what I tell you," I told the lad. "We always enter all the transactions at the end of the round."

"My shop steward knows how to do this job properly," the lad was telling me.

"You really are trying my patience," I told him.

"I don't care," he said. "I know how this round works, not you."

So I drove to the next road – he was grinning like a Cheshire cat – he thought, I got him, I've won. I was going to get him the sack when we got back to the yard.

In the next road he disappeared for twenty minutes. "Where the hell have you been?" I asked him.

"Having a cup of tea with a customer."

That was it, the end of the line for me. I got out of the van, shut the rear doors, put on the padlock, got back in the van and started off down the road.

"What are you doing?" he asked me, "we haven't finished the round."

"You have, son, I have just sacked you. I'm taking you back to the yard; I've had it with you. When I tell the boss just how cheeky you are and the rude comments you made and refusing to tell me what your customers have had, that's instant dismissal. I bet your shop steward never told you that, did he? And I am going to ask them to hold back your wages in case I come up short."

He went white. "I'm sorry, Dave, I'm sorry, honest I am. Let's finish the round please; I will do all you ask, and tell you what my customers have had when you ask me to. So I turned the van around and finished the round. For the next two weeks he turned out to be the best rounds boy I had ever worked with. Why he thought he could behave like that

I will never know – it wasn't his nature, so me shocking him the way I did bring him to his senses.

What's that I hear you asking? Did I have sex with that pretty lady who had seven kids? Well the very next day the checker came out with me asking all the customers if they were happy with the service they were getting, and if the quality of the goods were to their liking. I knocked on the door of the lady with seven kids. "I've been waiting for you; I've got it all ready to give you the time of your life." Then she noticed the boss was with me. "Is that the boss?"

"Yes," I told her.

"Damn, and I was really looking forward to today. OK, I will wait for you tomorrow," she said. "Trust me, you are going to have the time of your life."

The next day I was taken off that round and put to work on the deck because the rounds man had returned to work. Would I have? Well, we will never know.

I went to work for the Raleigh bicycle company for a short while after this job.

I got a new house in Chelmsley Wood, so I left Handsworth and handed in my notice at the bakery, well that's no surprise is it? Some time later I got a job at the Co-op bakery in Stechford, the same bakery I was at as a boy. I was only there two months, so I haven't written about it, nothing to write about that job really.

PITCH AND TOSS

Along the Chester Road in the area now known as Smiths Wood, Bryant's the builders had their compound. There, me and my brother John got a job. We were given a pair of Wellingtons, and a shovel to clean up the site. To start with we dug out drives and levelled out the shale for the pathways. There were no fancy diggers in those days, all the fetching carrying and levelling was done by hand. When the cement lorry and the brick lorry came in, they were unloaded by hand. The house bricks were the worst to unload, none of the labourers liked that job; we used to try to hide so we wouldn't be picked to unload it, but the site foreman knew this, and he knew when the lorry was coming in so he used to round us up before it got to the site. In those days the driver would climb onto the back of his trailer and throw the bricks to us, three at a time. Brick dust went in our eyes and that made one's eyes very sore for a good few days, sometimes even worse than that, the ends of our fingers used to get skinned and bleed, it was like getting an electric shock every time you touched anything. The firm never supplied gloves, no one would ask for any because the other workers would laugh at the person asking. It took about two hours to unload those brick lorries, sometimes even longer. I think that was the worst job to do on any building site.

Any road up, one afternoon we were in a house, me my brother and two other lads, and we started to play pitch and toss – one of us pitched a penny towards the wall, then the others would toss a penny to see if they could cover the penny or land on it, and the one that did land on it would be the winner. He would then claim the coins that had missed. If none of the coins was touching the first coin that had been pitched, we just kept tossing coins till one did land on the first one. Well, we got carried away; we were supposed to be working and the site foreman had been looking for us. When he caught us playing pitch and toss he sacked the four of us. The whole site heard about us and our little game – we were famous for a while.

RALEIGH BICYCLES

Just up the road from my house in Downing Street (no, not number 10, number 78) in Handsworth, was a well known firm called Raleigh, and they made bicycles. Well I went into their personnel department and said my famous speech, it's almost like I invented it I said it that often: "Have you got any vacancies please?"

"We have a position going in the maintenance department," I was told.

"That will do," I said to the young lady.

So out came the foreman, "So you are looking for employment, are you? And where have you worked before, and why have you chosen this firm?"

I hate those stupid questions, they were always looking for silly, clever answers, and I always refused to do that, so I always said, "There is nothing unique about me, I'm just a common person but you will not be disappointed with my work." I remember only twice being refused a job because I wouldn't give clever answers.

"Can you weld?"

"No," I replied.

"Would you like to learn?"

"Yes, I would," I told him.

So he took me to the maintenance shop, and introduced me to the welder. He told him I was starting in the morning, and asked him if he would train me up. He agreed so no problem there. I was shown all over the factory. "Are you happy to start in the morning?"

"Yes."

"Good, I will see you tomorrow then."

My wife was happy; she thought, well, we might get some money coming in for a few weeks.

Well I started, got my leather apron, goggles and face shield. The welder had worked there for ten years, he was good. "The hardest welding is gas welding, arc welding is easy," he told me. So he showed me how to set up for ark and gas welding. "Let's see how good you are? I want you to do some gas welding around eight inch steel tubes, this is the hardest of it all to do." so he did some to start me off, and then I welded that tube all the way round. "Well that's as good as I can do."

Pointing to some other tubes he said, "Those two tubes, let's see if it was a fluke." I did those as well as the first one. "You are a natural at gas welding," he said, and he showed me vertical gas welding, that's a little tricky but I was ok. "Well, arc welding you will do with no trouble at all." I found I couldn't do it, I kept getting the rod stuck. "I don't believe it, gas is the hardest to master, yet you took to it no bother, ark is easier and you can't do it, I'm amazed," he said to me. "Keep practicing, it will come to you," but it never did. I went all over that factory with my gas bottles, never the ark welder.

One day in the maintenance department I overheard him talking about his wages, I was shocked; I was getting the same money as he was and he was training me, I knew nothing. It was good for me, but not fair on him. I can't remember what my wages were, I remember lots of what was said to me and what I did when at each job but for some unknown reason I can't remember figures like the wages, I've tried, but I just can't remember. I started to get bored after two months so I handed in my notice.

MORRIS COMMERCIAL CARS

Morris Commercial Cars made the Morris Minor car and the van. This factory was situated in an area known as Bromford. Just across the road from this factory is Ward End Park where my dad fished for many years and I played as a child, and went to as a teenager on a Sunday in the summer in the hope of meeting my dream girl. I never did (ah). The Morris Minor was a wonderful and sturdy little vehicle.

I started at the Morris as a labourer sweeping up (money for old rope as the saying goes) all around the tracks. I watched with interest how things were done and put together, and when no one was about I had a go at doing the different jobs. I tried to get involved talking to the men, asking if I could have a go on the assembly line.

I was helping one day to lower the chassis onto the track, because I was a labourer I wasn't rushed like the men on the track. When any of the men needed the toilet I would say, "You go, I will carry on for you." If the boss or the shop steward had seen me doing what they classed as a skilled job, there would have been hell to pay – strange saying that, isn't it, hell to pay.

I asked the person who was putting in the two little back windows in the rear doors of the Morris van, "Can I have a go?"

"More than my job is worth," he replied.

"Go on, let's have a go."

"Oh go on then, but do it slowly, and be careful not to scratch the door," he told me. So I did a window. "Well done; that was very good," he said to me.

Every now and again I put windows in for him while he sneaked out for a smoke. This is easy, I said to myself, I'm getting good at this. But I got too big headed for my own good; I slipped one afternoon and put a scratch from the end of the window right to the top of the door. Needless to say, he wouldn't let me do any more, and I cannot print what he called me.

At the end of the track there were men called snaggers, they put right any mistakes that were made. When they saw the scratch they went, well...they were annoyed. It meant they had to move themselves and do some work and they did not like that.

I was transferred to the press shop, that part of the factory was called Nuffields. I was a labourer in that shop as well. I had a little electric truck that had bins on wheels towing behind it, those were for the scrap that came off the presses. When a bin at the side of the press was full I changed it for an empty one, then I took all the bins outside and tipped them out into a large bin that was taken away every so often to a foundry to be melted down. All the men on the presses were old hands, nobody left there unless they died.

One day four of us men were offered jobs on the presses, they had a large rush order so they created four new jobs, which meant four more jobs were available, so four men could get a job labouring. This is how it worked, on the presses, one man pushing a button, two men putting the metal sheet on the press, one taking off the scrap, while the two who put the sheet of metal on took off whatever had been pressed out. On some presses there were two putting metal on the press, two taking off the pressed out item on the other side of the press, and one pushing the button – pushing the button was the best job, the old hands always did that job, it was piece work, so no hanging about.

All the presses had a counter clock, this told the bosses how many times the press had gone up and down. If they never reached the quota and the boss wasn't around they would operate the machine without anything in it, in other words they were fiddling. Some of the clock counters had glass missing or broken, this helped the men to fiddle – with a pointed piece of metal they could change the number on it, showing more than they had done. When they did that, the men would stand on each corner of the machine to keep an eye out for the boss, if caught fiddling it meant instant dismissal, the union could not help under those circumstances.

I went on a machine one day and I asked one of the old hands to put me one hundred on the clock. It was a one man press. Unfortunately after about eighteen minutes the boss came to me and said, I need you on a big press." When he went to write down the amount I had done he scratched his head, called the head boss over and said, "Look at this, the machine does one hundred an hour, he hasn't been on it for half an hour, it's impossible to have that many on the clock."

I'm in trouble now I thought. I was thinking of all the excuses I could put my tongue to, when the head boss said to the other boss, "You must have forgotten to clear the clock."

"I didn't," he said. "I didn't, I know I didn't."

I just kept quiet, that made a change for me.

I had to work nights at Nuffield's, I did not like that at all. Thinking about it, I didn't like days either, ha, ha! I never went to work on a Monday because I was earning big money – I remember that wage, thirty two pounds a week when I worked nights; I always knocked Monday night off as well.

I was called into the office and the manager said, "You know what your trouble is, son? You are earning too much money."

"Too much?" I said, with a cheeky smile.

"If you knock any more nights off I will sack you."

Well that was a red rag to a bull was that. "Oh yeah?" I said, pulling a nasty looking face, don't bother yourself; lick em on – I'm off."

Talk about cutting your nose off to spite your face. When I got home I said to the wife, "I told em to lick em on.

"Not again, Dave!" she said.

I sat drinking my cup of tea and I thought to myself, well, if brains were made of dynamite I wouldn't have enough to blow my nose. Ain't that the truth!

CHELMSLEY HOSPITAL

I lived just across the road from Chelmsley Mental Hospital as it was known locally then, I got a job there working in the maintenance department as a fitter's mate. My role was to follow the fitter like I was a little puppy carrying his bag of tools. My title was known as a fitter's mate (fitter's get) get me this, get me that, whatever I was asked for by the fitter. Then one day my title changed from fitter's mate, to semi-skilled engineer, so incline your head, you are now talking to a man with a title – same job, same money, nothing changed only on paper. The job that was allocated to me was unblocking toilets on a daily basis, (well toilet attendant would have been a more appropriate title at that hospital) they always told me to unblock the toilets and that was continuously.

The boss came to me one day and said, "I want to see how good you are, I want you to go all around the wards and fix wire cages over the radiators, the rads get very hot and I don't want the patients burning themselves."

Strange, I thought, cages around the rads now when there has been nothing around them since the place was built in the 1930s, I believe, so I placed wire cages around every rad in every ward, it took me a long time; I didn't rush because I wanted to stay away from those toilets.

Another afternoon the boss came up to see how I was getting on. "Well done, David," he said in his posh voice (anyone that ain't a Brummie to me talked in a posh voice). He then asked me if I would like to learn about boiler houses.

"Oh yes," I replied; I wasn't the least bit interested really, I was just humouring him.

"Good, David, I'm very glad to hear that. With an attitude like that you will go far." Far? I thought, I'm only a fitter's mate, (oops, sorry, a semi-skilled engineer, don't you know). "Follow me," he said."

At the front of the hospital we went down a flight of steps into a boiler room. "There you are, two boilers. I would like you to clean them."

Well now that's how to learn about boilers, I don't think, I was thinking to myself.

"When the dirt is removed you can see what they look like."

As if I didn't know what a boiler looked like! OK, I thought, this will last a very long time, weeks in fact. I very quickly cleaned the brass and copper items so when he looked in to see how I was getting on it looked like I was working hard at my job.

"Oh splendid, splendid job, super, keep it up!" He was a very intelligent man; I was skiving and taking him for a fool and I thought I was being clever. Three weeks I was in that boiler house, sometimes I sneaked out and went home and had a three hour dinner break; well, all good things come to an end, so did that boiler job.

Then it was toilets to repair or unblock. When one afternoon we ran out of gasket paper which was used to repair steam pipes, I went with the fitter to the maternity hospital next door; both hospital were only divided by a high wooden fence running the full length of the grounds. We entered the maintenance department to scrounge some gasket paper, and I started to talk to the fitter, Tommy. "How are you getting on with Pipey?" that was my fitters nick name, his real name was Jack.

"Oh Jacks OK, it's the job I don't like. All I seem to do is unblock and repair toilets."

He laughed, "Why don't you have a word with our engineer, I need a mate to work with me."

"What's his name?" I asked.

"Bob."

So I walked around the maternity hospital, and after ten minutes I found the boss, Bob. I explained to him the situation – that I couldn't stand cleaning and repairing toilets anymore. "I don't blame you, I couldn't stand doing that either," he told me. "OK, look, don't say anything to anyone, just report here on Monday morning and I will square it with head office, but if your engineer gets wind of it, he will try to block it."

Come Monday I started working around the pregnant population of Birmingham – it was like coming off a tip to a holiday camp. The engineer did get wind of my transfer and tried to block it, unsuccessfully I'm glad to say.

MARSTON GREEN MATERITY HOSPITAL

I transferred from the Chelmsley Hospital on the morning I started working at the Marston Green Maternity Hospital. I found the atmosphere very calm and peaceful. My role at both hospitals was to carry the tools for the fitter, I was known as the fitter's mate, just the same as before (well semi skilled engineer).

All the wards at this hospital were surrounded by a corridor in such a way that it was in the shape of a horseshoe, so it was always referred to as the horseshoe. My job was to go all around that horseshoe every morning and put oil in the pumps that supplied the hot water to that particular ward. Every ward had its own pumping system for the central heating and hot water. On the roof of the laboratories was a huge extractor fan, I used to grease that fan after I had oiled all the pumps in the horseshoe, after that I had to work with whichever tradesman needed a hand. I worked with the electrician, the carpenter, the plumber, the builder, and of course the fitter and I learned a great deal from each one of those tradesmen.

All the steam pipes that fed the wards were old and prone to leaks; I was fascinated to see how those leaks were stopped. Whenever we saw steam puffing out of the pipes we would get what they called lead wool, bearing in mind those steam pipes were very hot, I would put some of the lead wool into the spot where the steam was escaping – I had a glove on of course, then with a screw driver I would ram the lead wool in place, then with a little hammer and a very small chisel I would tap it in till it was really rammed in, that is how we stopped steam leaks.

One afternoon I was working with the plumber – the main stop cock was leaking in a wards kitchen, it was fed by a lead pipe. That day I learned an operation I have never forgotten. It's not possible to lead wipe a joint when water is present, so with a nail the plumber put a hole a little away, underneath from the stop cock, this allowed a jet of water to escape out of that hole that stopped the water from reaching the stopcock, which allowed the plumber to lead wipe the joint using his blow lamp putting in some Talla fat to clean the joint. Then he melted the lead into the joint making it water tight, with a leather pad he smoothed the lead, that was known as lead wiping a joint. What really fascinated me was then with a match stick placed in the hole he had made with the nail, he placed a screw driver over the top of the hole, he taped down forcing some of the lead from the pipe to cover the matchstick and to my surprise the leak was stopped, that's how to lead wipe a leaking joint.

I bought two cottages in a little village. I had central heating put in, and I watched the plumber do exactly the same operation. When he found my stop cock had a leak I told him the plumber at the hospital did exactly the same thing. "Yes, that's how it is done," he replied.

"Have you ever had a leak from where you put in the matchstick?" I asked him.

"Never," he replied. "That will never leak as long as you are alive," he told me.

At the hospital, I was working with the carpenter, he was known as Clem because he looked just like an old Prime Minister, Clement Atlee, I did many jobs with him. He told me that originally the maternity hospital was built and used for the Canadian servicemen (women?) in the war, and the ballroom floor which was maple wood was supplied and fitted by the Canadians, as wood in this country was in short supply at that time.

One thing that may make you smile: there was an engineer that worked at the maternity hospital and he was a real snob. One afternoon he was telling me and the two men that worked in the stores, "A man walked past my house last night and he was scruffy," his face screwed up as he repeated himself, "yes, really scruffy and he walked past my house."

We all laughed and the Scottish store man said as he was holding his stomach while laughing and trying to get his breath, "If air was on ration he wouldn't let you anywhere near him."

Well, the engineer could not understand why we weren't agreeing with him. "Well you wouldn't like a scruffy man walking past your house would you?" He said as he walked away.

Marston Green Hospital

This map is showing the maternity wards, they were on both sides of what was known as the 'horse shoe' because of its shape. The map also shows the Chelmsley Hospital next door.

I worked in both these hospitals as a semi-skilled engineer

There was a tradition that was adhered to at that hospital: when a child was born there and it was time for mother and baby to go home, a nurse always carried the baby out of the ward to the awaiting transport, and then wished mother and baby good luck. My son and my four grandchildren were born at the Marston Green Hospital and that was a really nice tradition.

All Marston Green Hospital and most of Chelmsley Hospital next door have both since been demolished but part of Chelmsley Hospital is now Brooklands, and also there is an NHS crèche and some new houses have been built on the site. A lot of the buildings were saved and altered into dwellings and some into offices and it is known as Pinewood Business Park. The original chapel is still standing on that site.

MOTHER'S PRIDE

I went to work for Mothers Pride Bread, because it was a job working outside – I didn't want the job really, but it was three weeks before Christmas. I doubled up with another man till Christmas was over as he was leaving and I was taking over the round; the round was in the Studley area.

On Christmas Eve, just as we were approaching the depot at the end of the day the driver said, "I can drop you off here if you want so you can go home to your family – I will see to the van and the returns." The returns were the bread and cakes that were unsold. So I got into my van and went home. Great, I thought, spend more time with my family, when I suddenly remembered I hadn't picked up my wages – how can anyone forget to pick up their wages? I did. So I went all the way back from Chelmsley Wood to Bordesley Green where the bakery was situated near the city centre.

The supervisor smiled at me and said, "I thought I was going to have a great Christmas on you!"

I never opened that wage packet till after Christmas so I needn't have gone back for it.

When I started to deliver on my first week I was offered sex from a customer – no I didn't, I refused, I made them pay their bread bill!

After I had worked for Mothers Pride for one month, I was told to have a medical. It was a Thursday, I remember, pay day. When the doctor looked at my ears he asked, "How long have you had a perforated ear drum?"

"I was born with it," I replied. He dismissed me on the spot – well I didn't have to say, lick em on – I'm off, they did it first.

The Monday before, I had an armful of bread and cakes, and went to the car park only to find someone had stolen my van. A week later I went to a sweet shop just up the road from the bakery and I was telling the lady that someone had stolen my grey van. She in informed me there had been a grey van parked in the road at the side of her sweet shop. I went to have a look to see if it was my van, and to my surprise it was! I was wondering what had been stolen from it, but there was nothing missing, in fact it had been filled up with petrol, what's more I had been passing my van all the week travelling on the bus to work and back. Since then I have often wondered if they intended to use it for a robbery as it had stood there all week and was full of petrol.

Anyway, there I was – jobless again.

STEWARTS AND LLOYDS

This firm was based in the Bromford Bridge area of Birmingham. On the front of the building was a very long tube, this was facing the road so people passing could see it, it had a plaque above it saying, the longest tube in the world, or words something like that. They made all sorts of tubes, from lampposts to injection needles.

The firm on the other side of the road facing Stewarts was Rollason wire rolling mills, where Barry Farrington worked, he was my next-door neighbour.

Stewarts was a little different from other firms I worked for in as much as they insisted on the first day of your new job you had to do an introduction course. I found this to be a total waste of the firm's money, a drain on the firm's resources. There was about eight of us freshmen, plus two men taking the class that had worked there since they left school at the age of thirteen and fourteen, plus two young apprentices that were also employed there. We were given a talk on how and where the firm started and what they produced, and when that was over we had our dinner break. After dinner we were taken around the factory by the apprentices, we were given a hard hat and a pair of goggles and told when to put them on and take them off. It's got to be the most pathetic thing that's ever happened in my life. As we walked into one part of the factory we were told to put on our hard hats and goggles as there were men cutting steel and sparks were flying. So in we went, all looking like bandits, only to see that none of the men working in that department were wearing any kind of safety equipment – we found this throughout the factory.

Next day I was put working with two men rolling round long lengths of steel, twenty feet long and about eight inches in circumference. A man on the night shift had put a cut in these with a gas torch to the length required (most bars had four nicks in them). With six-feet round steel crow bars, two of us would bar one of those lengths of steel into a trough, then all three of us would put our crow bars as far under the long length of steel as possible and with a sort of rowing action we walked that length of steel along the trough under a machine, with the nick in the steel facing downwards, and a sort of arm would come down with a flat piece of metal, with the bottom of it shaped like a V –it looked like the blade of a bolster chisel. As it touched the steel with slow pressure and putting a few tons of pressure pushing downwards, the steel rose into the air; I bet it lifted three feet into the air, and when it snapped at the point where the nick was it fell back into the trough with a bang. We had to stand well away because sometimes it would bounce out of the trough and spin round. The trough was made of steel, very thick steel.

The other strange thing about that firm was there were more holes in the sides and the roof than you could shake a stick at. When the wind was blowing hard the rain or the snow, whichever was about at the time, made it very uncomfortable to work in those conditions, and to help you to not freeze altogether the firm in their infinite wisdom put braziers around the work shop with a pile of coke – in really bad conditions they were as much use as a teapot with no bottom in it. Any road up, one afternoon as I was barring one of those steel rolls towards the trough, because the floor was uneven the steel roll was slightly rising over a lump in the floor so instead of going over, it came back so all the weight rolled on to my crow bar. Pushing it down to the ground, with my hand underneath that crow bar, boy was it painful! The man who was barring with me had his bar wrenched from his hand as the weight of the steel roll went onto it; he very quickly got another crowbar to bar the steel roll off my hand. That was only in the 1960s; once again it was like working in the Dickensian era. I was off sick with my hand, and never got compensated for that accident. I handed in my notice while I was on the sick, so it was off to pastures new once again.

WONDERLOAF

Wonderloaf was a bakery company based in Wolverhampton and they rented a yard in Blake Lane in the Bordsley Green area of Birmingham. What that company were hoping to do was to break into the Birmingham area bread trade, of course that was impossible with the well established bread companies like the Co-op, Mothers Pride, Hawley's, Harding's, Wimbushes and Scribbens, plus many smaller companies like Braggs.

I started to work for Wonderloaf on a Wednesday, and I was immediately put on a round all around the Northfield and the Lickey Hills area. After a couple of weeks they had a competition selling Hovis. Out of one hundred and fifty calls, I got one hundred and fifty customers buying a Hovis loaf for a whole week. One by one they cancelled the Hovis orders till I was only selling two Hovis loaves a week. I came second but I could never find out who had won or how many loaves they sold. I went to Wolverhampton and I was asking all the rounds men if they knew who had won but no one would tell me, not even the head office; as I was an outsider I had my nose pushed out – I think I won that competition. Still, I got a boxed set of Parker pens which my wife loved.

Wonderloaf never got going in Birmingham, I for one stopped trying; to be honest I was putting the customers off – I lost a few. The calls were so spread out it was costing more in petrol and wages than the amount of goods I was selling; the wages were poor anyway.

One morning I noticed a tray of twenty four blackcurrant fresh cream cakes on my van, I hated those cakes, the boss said, "I've put those on your van because you never order any, that's because you don't like blackcurrant do you?"

"Nobody does, do they? Well when I bring them back unsold don't blame me," I told him. I sold them all in my first two roads, so after that he kept on putting fresh cream items on the van – trifles, cakes and sponges. The customers got fed up with them, and I started to take them back. He accused me of not trying; I even ate a few myself.

One day I had a dozen fresh cream trifles on, I was driving too fast, I hit a bump, and every trifle went into the air and turned upside down! I sold them at a quarter of their price that came out of my pocket.

I got really fed up with that job so I went off sick, but when I went back a week later I was called into the office by the boss and was told, "I'm letting you go, I don't think you want to offer any more of your time to the company; I think you have lost interest." He was so right. The daft thing was, a boy my wife knew through his mom-in-law (I didn't know him but I had put in a good word for him) worked on the side lines and they took him on and got rid of me. Oh well, I thought, new horizons here I come. That company only lasted a few months longer in Birmingham; they gave up the fight and went back to where they belonged, Wolverhampton. I don't think there are any firms now delivering bread and cakes door to door these days.

COCA-COLA

When I started at Coca Cola I had driven artics, three wheeled scammels for the railways, lorries of all sizes and weights, and an ordinary car licence was all one needed to drive lorries at that time. When I went to Coca Cola by this time the law had changed. If there were two axles on the rear of the lorry, you needed an HGV, heavy goods vehicle licence, class two. One axle and you had to have a class three licence. So the Coca Cola Company put me through a driving test for a class two licence. Their retail lorries at that time were only three tons max weight. So a class three was all one needed to drive their retail lorries.

On my interview for the job of salesman driver, a driver put his head around the door – he had just come from having his driving test – and the man interviewing me, Mr Frank Bunce, asked him how he had got on. "I've failed," he said. "He won't pass," he said pointing at me. He didn't know me; I was annoyed because I was on my interview, but he was upset because he had failed.

Frank knew, he said, "Don't worry about that." He asked if I had an HGV.

"No," I replied.

"That's all right; I will put you in for your HGV test."

Great, a heavy goods licence and I won't have to pay for it, I was thinking.

I started the next day. I was used as a rounds boy for the first week, I didn't even drive the lorry, they said they wanted me to get used to the job to see if I wanted to stay. I was working with a supervisor, his name was John. I did do some of the paper work, working out the bills for the customers, but the job was very hard and it carried a lot of responsibility – a lorry, lots of cash, a lorry load of pop, plus a rounds boy, and all my wages were at that time was £25.23p a week. I was delivering down alleyways, up and down cellars, up flights of stairs. Some of the cinemas were the hardest, three flights of stairs with two crates of pop in each hand, yes, very hard.

My H.G.V. Licence
Heavy goods vehicle
1972

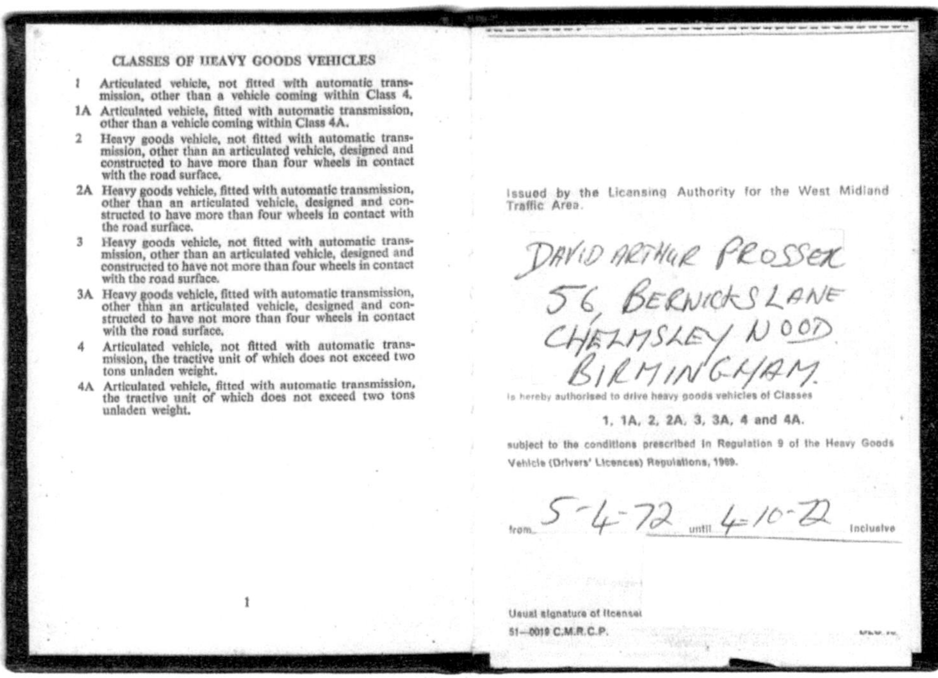

CLASSES OF HEAVY GOODS VEHICLES

1 Articulated vehicle, not fitted with automatic transmission, other than a vehicle coming within Class 4.

1A Articulated vehicle, fitted with automatic transmission, other than a vehicle coming within Class 4A.

2 Heavy goods vehicle, not fitted with automatic transmission, other than an articulated vehicle, designed and constructed to have more than four wheels in contact with the road surface.

2A Heavy goods vehicle, fitted with automatic transmission, other than an articulated vehicle, designed and constructed to have more than four wheels in contact with the road surface.

3 Heavy goods vehicle, not fitted with automatic transmission, other than an articulated vehicle, designed and constructed to have not more than four wheels in contact with the road surface.

3A Heavy goods vehicle, fitted with automatic transmission, other than an articulated vehicle, designed and constructed to have not more than four wheels in contact with the road surface.

4 Articulated vehicle, not fitted with automatic transmission, the tractive unit of which does not exceed two tons unladen weight.

4A Articulated vehicle, fitted with automatic transmission, the tractive unit of which does not exceed two tons unladen weight.

1

Issued by the Licensing Authority for the West Midland Traffic Area.

DAVID ARTHUR PROSSER
56, BERNICKS LANE
CHELMSLEY WOOD
BIRMINGHAM.

is hereby authorised to drive heavy goods vehicles of Classes

1, 1A, 2, 2A, 3, 3A, 4 and 4A.

subject to the conditions prescribed in Regulation 9 of the Heavy Goods Vehicle (Drivers' Licences) Regulations, 1969.

from 5-4-72 until 4-10-72 inclusive

Usual signature of licensee

51—0019 C.M.R.C.P.

My H.G.V. Licence
Heavy goods vehicle
1972

I went out one week with a driver, his round was different to all the others, he carried one gallon jars of concentrated Coca Cola, Fanta Orange and Fanta Lemon, and these were for the machines that were on the counters of cafes, restaurants and pubs. They were the type of machines where you put your cardboard cup against a lever. The syrup of Coca Cola would be mixed with soda water to give it the fizz, and when the cylinders needed filling, I would let the gas out of the cylinder, take off the lid and pour the syrup in. Those cylinders were stainless steel and held four gallons of the syrup; they were always under the counter, directly under the machine on the counter. I liked that round; they called it 'post mix'.

I went on many different rounds just to get used to all the different areas. I was working on a round in the Solihull and Shirley areas, the salesman was off sick. One morning I got the lorry loaded and went into the office to get the rounds book, those books had all the days of the week in them, the name of the shop and every customer on the individual day – on average there were thirty customers to serve a day, we called once a week to each customer. The summer was a different ball game, as the saying goes, that job became very hard. On very hot days the customers sold out very quickly so they would phone the office for an extra delivery. On those types of days there were never enough hours in the day to do the job, and some customers were never satisfied, no matter how good you were to them. The winter was really easy, some customers had only one delivery in six weeks, and then only two cases. There were twenty four small bottles of coke in each case, and with the post mix most customers in most cases had only one jar every four to eight weeks, when snow was about even longer. The wages were poor in the winter, and our bonus was very low.

One Monday morning I went to get the rounds book. Frank Bunce, the sales manager said, "Are you looking for the rounds book, Dave?"

"Yes."

"The supervisor is doing the round; you are having two days driving tuition. You are booked in for your test on Wednesday; I never told you Friday, I didn't want to spoil your weekend."

Frank was a nice man, he worked his way up from a delivery driver, and he did well for himself. Coca Cola is a very nice firm to work for.

I was waiting in the sales room for my instructor when Frank came in and told me my lorry had been checked over. "It's all ok, so it's ready for your tuition."

I drove it to the front of the building, and a little man got in and introduced himself to me. "I'm from the British School of Motoring B S.M, he said, then laid out on the seat all his licences and certificates. "These are to show you I'm very qualified and I know what I am talking about. I've taken all the vehicle tests and advanced tests that are going, OK?"

"Yes," I replied.

"Good, now start off, go to the end of the road, turn left and head for Stratford upon Avon; only turn left or right when I tell you to." Just before we got into Stratford upon Avon, he said, "Pull into the left by that lamppost and switch off, this is where we have breakfast."

Two hours later he decided I was going to get some tuition. We went to a disused airfield known as Long Marston, where there was a long run of concrete that used to be the runway. There were lots of cones already set out; it appeared that all lorry drivers used it when being given tuition. He reset the cones for different manoeuvres. I zigzagged in and out of the cones, and backed into a bay where the cones were set out in a sort of square to represent backing into a bay. He showed me the right way to do it; he drew a line. I was travelling at thirty miles an hour when he shouted, "Stop!" I hit my brakes. He got out and looked to see if I had stopped on the line. "Perfect, just do everything I've showed you and you will be OK on your test." So four times I did all the manoeuvres that he had shown me, and he was very happy. We then went back to the café and sat in there for three more long hours – I was bored sick.

The following morning the driving instructor strolled up nearly an hour late. "Are you all right, driver?" he asked.

"I'm fine, thank you."

"Good, come on then we are running a little late." We set off. "Drive to the café, driver, we will have breakfast." We sat in that café all day,

Doing a delivery of Coca Cola

never moved – brother was I bored, even more bored than the day before.

"Am I having any tuition today?" I asked him.

"No you don't need any."

I laughed. "You won't say that if I fail tomorrow," I told him.

"Look, if you needed it, I would take you out and give you some. Remember I told you I was qualified – and don't question me." So I apologized, I think I had upset him. "I have never had a driver fail yet." Yes, I had upset him. I hope I'm not the first to let him down, I thought.

Next morning I was feeling very nervous as we went to the testing station at Garrets Green. The examiner was a little bald round-faced man, with round wire framed specs, and he was wearing trousers that were too short for him – they came past the top of his boots. Oh no, I thought, he looks horrible. I did the test pad just like I had been shown, did the reverse zigzag, thirty mile an hour emergency stop, all OK. I was told to look in my mirrors every seven seconds so all over my test I was counting to seven, then left mirror, then right mirror, on to the road we go, throat dry, nerves all over the place.

"Pull over to your left please driver and stop." He looked at me and said, "Well."

"I'm sorry, I didn't hear what you said," I said to him.

"I didn't say anything; cancel your indicator."

That's it, I thought, he will fail me for that, so I took a deep breath and thought to hell with it, if I fail, I fail, he knew I was nervous. I was told to pull away so I drove like he wasn't there. "Turn only when I tell you to, driver." Well I drove and drove, I went through Stratford, I glanced at him a couple of times, I'm sure he is asleep, I was thinking, by this time I had been driving for nearly an hour, so I coughed loudly and his head came up with a jerk. "Oh, erm...take the next right, please, driver," he said. By the time I got back I had been on that test just over two hours, and I felt drained. He looked at me, smiled and said, "That was a beautiful drive, thank you, driver."

Then questions on the highway code followed. "I'm pleased to say you have passed."

"Would you like six bottles of coke?" I asked him. "I wouldn't ask you before in case you thought I was trying to bribe you." He shoved them in his briefcase like he was scared I would take them back. I shook his hand and off he went. I don't like Coca Cola myself but I opened one and it went down so sweet – I needed it, my throat was so dry.

My tutor came up to me, congratulated me on my pass then said, "Where the hell have you been, you should have been back over an hour ago?" I explained I thought he had gone to sleep. He laughed, "See, I told you you were a good driver." Easy to say that after the event isn't it?

I got that round selling the gallon jars of coke (you know the post mix I was telling you about); I loved that round. I delivered to the Shakespeare Theatre in Stratford upon Avon, and Winston Churchill's place of birth, Blenheim Palace. I went to all the main towns, Oxford, Banbury, Leicester, Stratford, Birmingham, Leamington, Rugby and many more.

Every year come Christmas we had the chance to win a hamper, it was a team effort. All the rounds were involved, including the management. There were spirits of all kinds, big tins of ham, tins of fruit and a thirteen pound turkey. We won the top hamper every year, every salesman got one – the turkey only just fitted in our oven!

The insurance cover that Coca Cola gave to all their staff was second to none; if I died while in there employ for whatever reason at home or at work, my funeral would be all paid for by the company and my wife would receive a few thousand pounds.

When I joined the Territorial Army I was paid full wages, plus bonuses no matter how long I was away, wonderful company, plus I got paid by the Army as well. I left that company because they went to telephone sales so I became a delivery driver, no longer a salesman. Want a shock? I worked there for three and a half years and never lost any time, and then I went to a firm called Goverbrook Loft Conversions.

GOVERBROOK

Goverbrook was a firm that did loft conversions. I went to see Bill, the owner, in my Coca Cola lorry; this lorry was a 25tonner, one big old fashioned lorry, wooden cab, no power assistance, horrible to drive. The boss of Goverbrook came out to look at it. "Good God, I never knew they still had lorries like this on the road." It was definitely a museum vehicle in my opinion.

"I heard you were looking for a driver." he looked surprised as I said it.

"How did you find that out?" he asked.

"You have a relation working at Coca Cola, I told him. I know the foreman here; he worked at Coke alongside me.

"Oh you mean Friar Tuck – we call him that because of his size."

I laughed, "We called him Polly because he never stopped talking."

"You can start Monday if you want to," the boss said.

"I have to give a fortnight's notice," I told him.

Bill agreed. "OK, that's all right, see you in a fortnight."

So after my delivery that day, I gave in my two week's notice. When Friday afternoon came, I got back to the yard, loaded the wagon for Monday, handed in my sheets, and the sales manager said, "I've paid you a fortnight's money in lieu, plus bonuses, holiday pay and what they owe you – over £400." So I had a nice week off before I started work for Goverbrook.

I started on the Monday; it felt very strange working with timber after carrying crates of pop for three and a half years. This job was easy, all I had to do was load up the timber, take it to the customer's house, and unload it – it was always put in the garden. I carried a large roll of plastic, which I cut to the length of the timber covering it all so it wouldn't get wet.

I was very interested to learn how to construct a loft conversion, and I asked questions all the time. I got to know about all the different materials needed to convert a loft. This is easy, I thought. I built a garage on the side of my house, and I got all the timber from work nice and cheap. The brother of a lad I went to school with was a bricklayer, and he laid the bricks and helped to put the roof on the garage; he taught me a lot. He got me all the bricks from a job he was doing. The carpenter at work made the door frame for my up and over door.

I worked a lot around Stoke on Trent; I delivered many loads of timber around Stoke and Bristol, Tamworth, Coventry, many, many places. Worcester was a favourite run for me. After a few months our boss was going broke. He sent me to Telford to pick up a cheque. "Be as quick as you can, Dave," he said, "so I can get it in the bank so I can pay your wages." I got nicked for speeding. "Don't worry, Dave, I will pay the fine for you, thanks for being quick," Bill assured me – too right I was quick, I wanted my wages. It did make me wonder just how broke he was, if he needed a cheque that badly. It turned out he was desperate, he had six teams, two men to each team.

The following Friday as I was loading up my wagon, a team of two men walked in. "Is Bill in his office?" they asked me.

"Yeah, he has just walked in, well ten minutes ago." They looked very angry. "What's up?" I asked.

"What's up? The cheque he gave us for our wages has bounced," they told me.

Oh my God, it's worse than I feared, I was thinking. I heard the boss say, "Morning lads," as though there wasn't anything wrong. I heard lots of shouting; they were saying, "We ain't doing another stroke on the loft we are on till we get our money."

"I will pay you this afternoon, lads," Bill told them both.

"Yeah, and we want cash, not a cheque," the both men were demanding. So off they went.

The boss called me into his office. "Take the lorry Dave to Bristol Street Motors in Perry Bar for a service; tell them you will wait for it."

I walked in."Hi, I'm from Goverbrook, I've brought the lorry for a service."

"Park it there," said the boss of Bristol Street Motors, pointing to a corner, "and give me the keys." I gave him the keys. "Right," he said, "that lorry is going nowhere till your boss pays us what he owes us."

Not again, I thought, so I phoned up the boss. "Bill, they won't give me the lorry back till you pay the bill."

I handed the phone to the boss. I heard Bill shouting, "I've got money, how dare you hold my lorry!"

"Well, just get down here and pay the bill."

With that, Bill came to the garage and paid them with a cheque. Things were getting really bad. The lady in the office told me to find another job as the firm had no money. That was the last time I saw her, she left. I got my wages in a packet as normal, it was a cheque, and yes, it bounced. I was very angry. I went in to the office and had a go at him. "Sorry, Dave, here you are, my personnel cheque."

"I want cash, Bill, not a cheque."

"It's OK, Dave, it will cash, it's out of my own account."

That bounced as well, so in the office I went. "I know Dave, here is another cheque made out to cash."

"It had better cash, Bill, it's nearly two weeks since I had any money and I have two children."

"It's OK, Dave, honest it will cash." So I took it straight home to my wife, she took it to the bank, and yes, it cashed.

I went in on the next Monday and Bill said, "Dave we are now called Dormer Construction, Goverbrook has gone into liquidation. So Goverbrook had finally got taken over by a timber firm in Dudley. They owed lots of money to that firm I never heard how much, I have no idea. So I teamed up with a carpenter named Barry who was a loft converter. I did a few lofts with him all over the country. We slept in the back of his van on the hard floor in a sleeping bag. It was winter and very cold; when I woke up in the morning the inside of the van was white with frost. I opened my flask and drank an ice-cold cup of tea. What the hell am I doing this for? I asked myself. I was working very hard carrying all the timber, plasterboards and eight by two floor chipboard up a ladder, never Barry, always me. I had no money, so I took a loaf and butter and jam; Barry had some of my bread, so half way through the week I wasn't eating at all. I found carrying the materials up the ladder getting harder by the hour, as I got weaker and my head was aching and I had no pain killers. Barry said, “I have only enough money to buy my meals,” so I sat every evening watching him eat a roast dinner. They had a shower in the place he ate at, and I asked him to lend me ten pence for the shower. “I ain’t got ten pence, Dave,” he said. “I wanted a shower and I can’t have one either.”

So I went back and sat in the van. Barry came back. “I see you had a shower then, Barry, I thought you hadn’t any money left.”

“Oh I found ten pence in my pocket,” he said.

“Well you ate my bread and jam and left me with nothing. Well I’m finished with you when this loft is finished, you ain’t a nice person to work with – we are supposed to look after each other.” Barry only thought about himself.

By the way, that fine – Bill never paid it; one Saturday morning I was got out of bed by a police officer and arrested and taken to the police station. I was bailed, and I told Bill on the Monday. He laughed, said it was still in his drawer – he had forgotten all about it! He did pay it that same day.

GOING ABROAD

I remember this journey to Italy very well because a few funny but scary things happened to us on the way back.

Andrew, who I went all over Italy with before, came to me one Friday afternoon and asked me if I would go to Italy with him and share the driving. In Chelmsley Wood there lived an Italian man who was married to an English lady; they had been living in Italy for a long time and decided to come and live in England. Andrew was asked if he would hire a furniture van and collect all the items of furniture from a flat in Milan. The couple travelled that Friday back to Italy so they were there before we arrived. Andrew knew I wouldn't refuse a free trip so it was all agreed before he asked me to go.

On and off the ferry, no problems, through France I was driving great, I thought. As we approached the start to the Alps I shook Andrew who was asleep at the time. "What are all those signs meaning?" I asked him.

"I don't know," he replied, "just carry on up over the mountain road." The road looked like it was super glued to the side of the mountain. Well it was getting dark, I drove and drove till it got light, and then we came to a lodge, which turned out to be the border control. Not a soul was in sight; there were a lot of barriers across the road and round the buildings – it turned out there had been a rock fall and the mountain road leading into Italy was closed for repairs, so all the way back down we went, it was one hell of a drop from that road to the ground. We wasted a lot of diesel that day just because the sign wasn't in English, as well as French, I was glad to get off that mountain road.

Any road up we made it to the destination and loaded up the lorry. "May I have a shower?" I asked, the man whose furniture we were collecting. The shower was turned on for me, but it went bitter cold, the water that is. After I got dressed I told them the water was freezing.

"Oh no," the man said, he couldn't apologize enough, "you know that lady who lives in the bottom flat, she is not nice, she thinks she owns the place. I bet she has turned off the hot water in the basement." And that is exactly what she had done.

Andrew had his shower, and he started to play me up, saying, "That was a lovely hot shower I had."

The young man, whose name I can't remember, took us to a restaurant to try proper Italian spaghetti, it was very nice.

It was about four in the afternoon, if my memory serves me right, maybe a little earlier, when we started back for England. It turned out we didn't know our vehicle was over three tons, lorries over three tons were not allowed on the roads at weekends. When we reached the Swiss border we were asked by the border guard, "What are you carrying?" We told him furniture and showed him the list. "Is he an Italian that is moving to England?"

"Yes," we told him. He pulled a face and asked, "For goodness sake, why?"

"For work," we explained, "for a better living than he can get in his own country." We were being sarcastic.

"You have to pay taxes of one hundred pounds now, or I will take the lorry off you," we were told by the guard.

Andrew was having a fit, he explained to me, "We will only just about have enough for our meals and the toll roads if I have to give him one hundred pounds, we might even be short!"

"It's OK Andrew, I've got fifty quid on me," I told him.

So as he turned towards me, away from the border guard, he slipped some notes under the seat, and with a fifty pound note and a couple of tens and some fivers, he fanned the money in his left hand, turned to the border guard and said, "This is all I've got and we have to pay the tolls."

The border guard reached in, snatched the fifty pound note and said, "That will do." He went into his shed and brought out a receipt, went to the back of the lorry and put a seal on it so we couldn't open up the back of the lorry, then he told us, "Over three tons, no travel on roads till Monday morning, so go round the corner and park up."

We had to get back to England or the lorry hire would cost us more money. As we turned the corner I said, "I will drive on Andrew, we will say we are only just three tons in weight if stopped."

The roads were almost deserted. As we passed the occasional motorist we got some funny looks. Just before we got to the next border I took the wrong turning, and I went through I think it was the Belgium border. I did a sharp turn about and put my foot down. The guard came running out with his pistol in his hand – that was a scary moment.

We got to the next Swiss border as they were just changing the night shift to the day shift. Well the look on their faces, it was too early for them to want to bother with us, the guard only asked how heavy we were. I told him, "Three tons."

He waved his hands, he wasn't interested in our paper work, "Go, go" he was saying, "Go, go," and go we did – very fast, well as fast as we could. We sighed a sigh of relief! In France you can drive to the ferry, but not from the ferry on weekends if you are a commercial vehicle. All went well from then till we got home; it was quite an adventure, I enjoyed it.

MAXIPOPS

Maxipops was a mineral water wholesale company, based in the Chelmsley Wood area of Solihull, near the N.E.C. Only wholesale companies were allowed to purchase their product. I absolutely hated working for this company. Most of the workforce came from the firm Corona, I believe Corona went into liquidation, but I'm not altogether sure about that. Their pop was, I thought, the best on the market, any road up, my job was to deliver to the shops around the Coventry area. Trying to work out their road system in Coventry was a day's work in itself. I had a rep working with me; he was good at his job.

We decided one day as it was coming up to Christmas, we would go all out, push the sales to make our wages better, as we were aware that after Christmas all we would be doing was picking up empties, and not such good wage packets. Off our own backs we were doing deals – if they only wanted one case, we would say, if you buy ten we will only charge you for nine, or buy ten cases we will give you one free; if they took fifty cases we gave them six cases free. The firm had an incentive scheme where we were allowed to give two free cases away, but not the amount we gave away. How the rep worked it, I have no idea, all I know is we sold thousands of cases in that three weeks, and our wages were very good for Christmas. We even swapped bottles of pop for bags of nuts and tins of sweets. After Christmas all we did was pick up empties, the bosses were none too pleased.

One very foggy morning I filled up the diesel tank and started towards Coventry. As I was going down a hill towards Stone Bridge Island, that's just down the road from the N.E.C. and the Birmingham Airport, a lorry had been dropping scrap metal onto the road. I saw it at the last minute because of the fog; I tried to avoid running over it, but the shape of the metal was boomerang, and I caught it with the inside of my tyre. It made a lot of noise as it hit the underside of my lorry. I turned to the rep and said, "That metal will cause an accident if it's not picked up." Visibility was only about ten yards so I couldn't stop to pick it up. As all drivers know it takes a lot of concentration when driving in fog. When I got to my first call I was facing uphill, and as I jumped out of the cab I saw diesel running down the hill from under my lorry. On close inspection I noticed a hole in one side of the tank and a hole on the other side of it. To say we were gobsmacked would be an understatement, but we were, that piece of metal I had hit had spun, gone through my diesel tank and out of the other side. Diesel is like ice when on the road so we phoned the fire brigade who came out about an hour later. In the meantime we had phoned the depot, told them the problem, and they sent out a mechanic with a new tank and twenty gallons of diesel. On arriving he told me that on the road where the diesel had come out of the tank because the metal had ruptured it, there had been a massive pile up – lorries and cars all skidding down the hill till they all met at the bottom. Among the vehicles, in his week old car was Sir Robert McAlpine. His car was squashed between two lorries. The mechanic said, "No one knows it was you that spilt that diesel."

"Well I'm phoning the police," I told him. "The firm is insured and those people have a right to compensation." I gave them the facts on how it happened, and then went about my business delivering the pop. On that Friday evening, on returning to the depot a little late, all the office staff had gone home so I couldn't hand in my log book.

On returning back to the depot on the Monday evening, I felt really rough with the flu. Just as I was about to enter the road where my depot was, I was stopped by a police car. "Let's have a look at your log book, you buggers never bother with them half the time," he remarked."

A lady police officer that was with him remarked how ill I looked. "I just want to go home to bed," I told her.

"You will go when I'm finished with you," the male officer said to me. He booked me for not handing in my log book Friday evening. I told him the offices were locked when I got back Friday so I was about to hand them in as soon as I got in that evening. I hadn't signed that day's sheet, so he booked me for not signing that day's log and not handing in last week's log sheets. I pointed out on the back of the log sheets that it states, if you are not able to hand in your log sheets do it at the next earliest possible convenience, but he wasn't interested, he still booked me. I wrote to the courts and explained what it said on the back of the log book and they weren't interested either – I got fined ninety pounds. A couple of weeks after that I handed in my notice; again I joined the ranks of the unemployed.

Nearly twelve months later a solicitor came to my house and asked if I would go to court as a witness about the accident. He explained they had offered a quarter of a million pounds, but Sir Robert McAlpine had refused, said it wasn't enough to pay for all the damage that had been done to all the vehicles involved in the crash. I didn't have to appear, but I was told, "We can't win without you."

So into court I went and sat and listened to all the owners of the smashed up vehicles. The barristers with white wigs and black gowns on truthfully were making me very nervous; I had to stand in front of them. After lunch the rep and the young lad that was with us at the time had a slap up lunch, I wasn't allowed to talk to them. I hadn't any money on me, so I sat on my own with one piece of toast and a cup of tea. As I walked into the dock I was grilled by their barrister. I'm not having this, I thought, so with a deep breath I piped up and said, "Excuse me, your honour, I'm only a common person, I just don't understand the big words the gentleman is saying to me, would you please ask him to talk to me in common English," which he did. After I had explained that if I hadn't have phoned the police no one would have known it was my lorry whose diesel tank had split, the case was dismissed. That insurance never paid out a penny.

I went into the solicitor's office; he shook my hand and said, "You were brilliant, you saved our company a lot of money."

"How much do I get?" I asked him.

His reply to me was, "Nothing, that would be against the law," and he gave me my bus fare home. If I had known then, what I know now, if they weren't going to pay me at least a day's wages, I would have refused to testify on their behalf – they really should have paid up to those people whose cars were damaged; that's why we have insurance.

WG.440.

WEST MIDLANDS POLICE

Our Ref : L1670/79

Your Ref :

Dated : 22 April 1980

From :

Superintendent
Eastern Traffic Sub-
Division
Homer Road
Solihull B91 3QL

Mr. D. A. Prosser
102 Orton Road
Warton
TAMWORTH
Staffordshire

Dear Sir

I am directed by the Chief Constable to say it has been reported to him that

~~on Tuesday~~, 20 November 1979, you deposited diesel on the A452 Chester Road, without lawful authority or excuse.

It is not proposed to take any further action on this occasion.

Yours faithfully,

Chief Superintendent.

A letter I got from the police after the accident on my way to Coventry in my lorry to deliver Maxi Pop to the shops. They made it sound like I went with a can and poured diesel all over the road. I did smile when I received it.

COUNCIL

Working for the council made me wonder why the bosses were not stricter with the workforce – one could get away with such a lot. I used to dodge the bosses to get out of working; don't get me wrong, the bosses were a very nice bunch of men. How I came to be working for the council was, one day I walked into the unemployment office in Chelmsley Wood and asked if any new jobs had come in that weren't yet on the board. "Would you do any type of work?" I was asked. "We have a temporary job with the Solihull council."

"Yes, no problem."

"The council are very short staffed at the moment, what with sick leave and holidays. I see you are a lorry driver HGV class two."

Yes, I am," I replied.

"Here is a letter, take it to a Mr Lightfoot at Moat Lane, Solihull."

As usual I wasn't concentrating (That's always been a problem of mine). I went to the council yard in Coleshill, well, no good being thick and not showing it, and handed in my letter. "This is fine; can you start in the morning?"

"Yeah, no trouble."

He knew I had gone to the wrong council so he took advantage of it because he was short staffed as well.

"We start at six a.m," the boss told me. Six a.m! I hate getting up in the mornings.

Well, I got there, only just, I might add, and I was introduced to a gang of men. "You will be working with these men."

"What am I driving?" I asked.

"No, you are not driving; you will be working on the refuse lorry emptying the bins." A dustman, I thought, no way – I came to drive lorries. I did go with the gang though, We went to Kingshurst, to pick up a man, and he strolled out like he was the boss. The driver had only been with the council a week, and I found that the four men sat in the back of the cab had taken a dislike to him. I had no idea why, they laughed and took the micky out of him behind his back. We were emptying bins all around the Marston Green area that day, and I was talking to the driver, he seemed OK to me. The crew were running around like wild things, I asked the driver," Why are they running around like wild things?"

"To get finished," he replied.

"What happens then?" I asked him,

"Nothing, we sit around till gone three, and we can then go back to the yard."

"But why run around like idiots, when it could be done almost as quick by walking fast?"

"I know that, try telling them. We would only take about an hour longer," he said. "I asked them that when I started last week, they said 'Toe the line and don't try to change things.'"

I asked, "How come we picked that fellow up this morning, why doesn't he come to the yard like the rest of us?"

"I'm not sure, he seems to tell the bosses what to do," he told me.

Next morning, same again, only this time we waited almost twenty minutes for the man to come out of his house. He said, "Morning lads, I got up late."

I thought I'm not having this, this will be my last day, I don't like this job and the bins smell something awful. One bin, I remember, had lots of waste food in it, and was crawling with maggots, thousands of them – I don't think they had emptied it for a long time. They missed bins, dropped rubbish all the time and never picked it up, they really were a law unto themselves. I don't know what hold they had over the bosses but they seemed to do just what they liked. We finished at eleven thirty that day and hung about.

When we did finally get back to the yard, I clocked out and shot over to Moat Lane depot where I should have gone in the first place. I went to see the boss, Mr Lightfoot, and there was another boss there named Sam, I can't remember his surname. I explained the mix up. "I'm not doing those bins anymore; have you a driving job or do I leave?"

"I have a driving job for you – that boss at Coleshill, he should have sent you to me; he tried to keep you because like us he is short staffed.

I will phone him and tell him you have transferred over to me, and I will sort your money out for you. The driving job I have is emptying the cess pits."

My God, I thought, out of the frying pan and into the fire! "Yes, that will be fine," I told him.

"Good, I'm desperate for drivers; all the customers are overdue for emptying."

It was expected that you empty six cesspits a day; I had a driver's mate, Dougie, working alongside of me. It was most certainly different to anything else I had ever done. The sewage farm was situated in Friday Lane, Barston, near Balsall Common. Come dinnertime I said to Dougie, "Where do you go for dinner?"

"We stay at the sewage farm where we empty our loads."

"Go on, you are kidding me, ain't ya?"

"No, what makes you think that?"

"Eat my sarnies with this smell around us?"

"What smell?" he asked me. "What do you mean? What smell, are you having me on?"

We were emptying our load as I was talking to him. I pointed to the sewage that was passing us at about thirty miles an hour. "That smell that comes from that," I said to him.

He put his head under the railings with his nose about two and a half feet from the sewage, took a really good sniff, looked at me and said, "I can't smell anything."

With a rubber hammer we uncoupled the pipes, put them away on the side of the tanker, sat in the cab and ate our sarnies. Dougie opened his sarnies, held one in his mouth while he poured out his tea from a flask, put his feet on the dash board, opened his newspaper and never uttered a word for the whole of our lunch break. I was feeling a little sick at the thought of eating my lunch in a dirty cab in a sewage farm, I tried, but I couldn't face it, so I drank my tea. I thought the dust carts were bad enough, but this!

I worked there a few months, I even enjoyed doing it after a couple of days, and yes, I ate my lunch at the same spot every day, where at first I couldn't, and believe it or not after a couple of weeks I too could not smell that sewage – they say you get used to anything in time, that is so true.

Apart from going around to little villages, we went to some beautiful little cottages that stood in little gardens on their own. To my surprise they had an outside toilet, you know the type, they had a plank with a hole in it with a bucket under the plank – those cottages didn't have a cess pit. I had to carry the bucket to the tanker and pour it into an aperture that was designed especially for that operation. At the back of the tanker I turned on a valve that would suck up all the waste that was put in it, it then entered the main body of waste in the tanker. I then replaced the bucket back in the correct position, that was one operation I defiantly did not get used to. When I returned to the back of the tanker there was a little hose pipe fixed by the aperture, and when the pump was turned on there came a strong jet of water from the hose, which allowed me to wash away any waste that was clinging to the sides. People that lived in the countryside in those days were subsidised till it changed overnight. The charges went from fifteen shillings a load, to seven pounds a load – they were angry, I can tell you; a lot of them let their cess pit overflow and soak away through the soil. One man I was talking to was throwing in a bucket attached to a rope, and when he retrieved it he watered his vegetable garden with it. I declined the offer of free veg from him. I don't think it's legal to use sewage to water the garden, and anyway, I wouldn't recommend it. I was asked many times if I would do a load half price with no ticket, of course I refused (I didn't have many friends when I did that job, ha ha); talk about Dickensian times, and that was in the 1970s when I was emptying buckets of waste.

SOLIHULL COUNCIL

When I was working temporary for this council helping out in the bin lorry, I was asked if I would work for them permanent, driving a new road sweeper. Why not, I thought. It was very small and it sounded like a jet engine when it was put into the sweep mode – I had to wear ear defenders it was so noisy. I was asked to go around the Solihull area to try it out, so I went into a grove where there were lots of leaves on the road and they were damp, but it would not pick up wet leaves. As I was running up and down that grove a lady came over to me and started to bang on the door of my sweeper – she asked me if I would go away as her husband was very ill, that tells you how noisy it was. So I tried other roads, but it was the same, I made more mess than there was there before. Back to the yard I went and explained it was a useless tool. It turned out it was made to sweep around shopping precincts for dust and bits of paper, not roads. It was broken down more than it was used, so I doubled up with a crew going around, sweeping the streets for a short time.

The winter came, and I was driving a snow plough at night, and gritting the icy roads, and in the day time I even drove a lorry with a gang of men cleaning up the town centres of different areas. I drove the cesspit lorries in the Meriden area of Warwickshire countryside, emptying the cesspits and taking them to the sewage farm in Barston lane, Solihull, that is mentioned in another chapter in this book. I even worked in the yard at times.

One day I took the team out to sweep the roads up by hand, I then returned to the yard. I wanted to leave early as it was my anniversary, but the boss was in a bad mood that day, for what reason I have no idea. He started to have a go at me, saying no one cared enough about their jobs enough. That was it, I said, "Lick em on – I'm off." That was the last time I worked for that council.

EAST BIRMINGHAM HOSPITAL

My wife, Irene, worked at this hospital, so did my sister, Doreen, they both worked there for some years. I got a job there as a driver-porter, and I remember that interview very well. I was asked if I could drive their little three-wheel artics. “Yes, I have a licence from the railway to drive those,” I told them.

I was taken to a quiet spot where there was a large concrete pad. There were two doors in the building, about five feet apart, and the head porter got into the cab and reversed it up to one of the doors, parking it across the doors, then he asked me to drive away, then back it up to the same door, as he had done. So I did it perfectly. I thought, after all these years I still have the knowhow.

He laughed and said, “That was great, and dead straight – I can see you have done it before.” My chest came out, I felt good. He said, “Trouble is, you backed up to the wrong door.” I felt such an idiot. Still laughing, he said, “It doesn’t matter, you have got the job.”

I had to work shifts, weekends as well. Every dinnertime when the kitchens had leftovers from the restaurant, us porters were given them; needless to say I ate very well while I worked there and piled on the pounds.

One of my duties was to go around all the wards collecting drugs and specimens. Another duty was to collect the dirty laundry, boy some of those bags stunk – those nurses deserve medals. Another duty was to take bodies to the mortuary, or Rose Cottage as it was known, we also had to take dinners to the wards, then collect the dirty dishes, if that wasn’t enough we were used as security guards as well! We were taught to do cardiac massage, but I’m glad to say I never had to do any of that for real. I also changed oxygen cylinders and delivered them to the wards; it’s a very worthwhile job but it wasn’t for me (what was I wonder?).

I had to go in on Christmas day, and I missed my two children opening their presents; I missed seeing the excitement on their faces as they tore open the presents – that hurt.

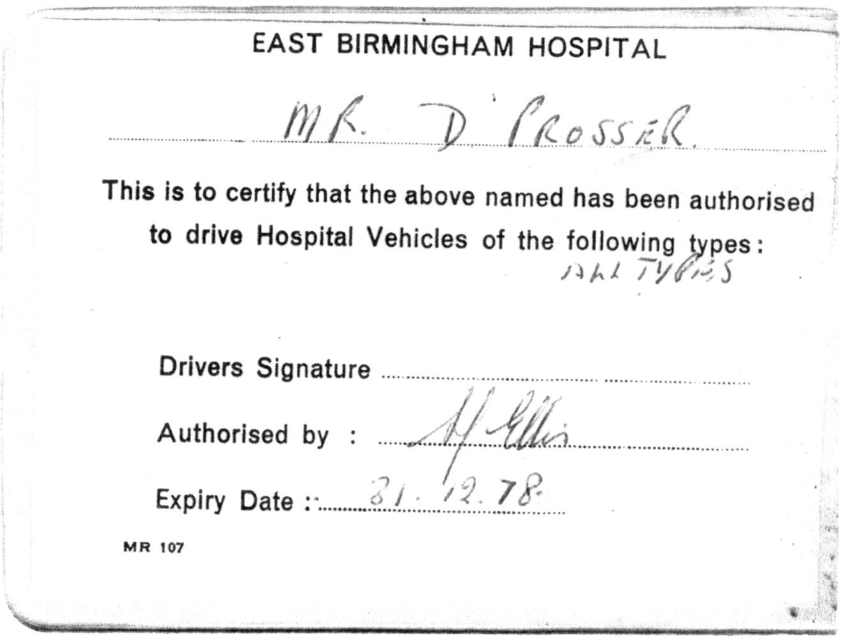

EAST BIRMINGHAM HOSPITAL

MR. D PROSSER.

This is to certify that the above named has been authorised to drive Hospital Vehicles of the following types:

ALL TYPES

Drivers Signature ....

Authorised by : ....

Expiry Date : 31.12.78

MR 107

My East Birmingham Hospital Driving Licence
(now known as Heartlands Hospital)
My Mom always called it Little Bromwich Hospital.

I transferred to the maintenance department, and I was literally all over the hospital then, seeing to pumps, attending to leaking steam pipes, even plumbing. I spent most of my time hiding and skiving – no walkie-talkies or mobiles in those days – when the boss was looking for me, he hadn't a chance of finding me. When he said he'd been looking for me and mentioned different places in the hospital, I would say, "Oh, by that time I was somewhere else, doing something else." It was easy to lie and get away with it. Nowadays it wouldn't happen, not with mobiles on the scene.

"Oh, never mind," the boss would say.

All the maintenance men did it, I bet there is still a way of hiding, there always is.

New adventures calling, I handed in my notice; I'd done about five months. Hospitals – definitely not my cup of tea, mind you, no job ever was.

D AND G SUPPLIES

When I left East Birmingham hospital (my mom always called it Little Bromwich, and many years ago it was known as the fever hospital) I got a job driving a Luton van for a firm known as D and G Supplies. They sold plumbing materials, bathrooms and kitchens.

After a very short time I was asked to sell bathroom suites on Saturdays, I enjoyed that, it was a challenge. I tried to excel as a salesman. I'm ashamed to admit when a customer was looking around the sales room, I would very slowly walk up to them and say, "Is there any one bathroom suite you like more than the others?" I got to tell which customers were really interested. I did get it wrong a few times, but in the main I won the day. I was not on a bonus or any extra wages, I just really enjoyed helping out the customers. I got a kick out of it when I got a good sale, the only little white lie I told them was, whatever bathroom suite they picked, I would say, "How strange is that? I've just bought that same one, I had it fitted last week; it looks lovely in situ." I would steer them away from the cheap, rubbish one. The one thing I do remember was the name, Sherrington; we had a cheap one and a dearer one – one was ten ml. thick and the other was only eight ml. thick, but they looked identical, so I always told the customer how to tell the difference.

One Saturday afternoon a lady went to the owner, my boss, and said to him, "Your salesman, Dave, is the most polite and well mannered salesman I have ever come across." That was my third Saturday as a salesman with that company. Another Saturday I was talking to a couple who had their two children with them, why I remember how many of them there were, I have no idea, the only thing I can think of was it was because of the man. How it worked at that time was, I would sell the goods, hand the paperwork over to the boss, and he would work out the discounts and the total cost. This particular day we were very busy, that family spent over a thousand pounds, and I took the paperwork to the boss.

"Dave," he said, "you do it, I'm very busy."

So I sat down and filled out the bill, did the discounts and costed it all out. As I looked up the man was looking really concerned. "Everything OK, sir?" I asked him.

"Well," he replied, "you working that out in your head..."

Hs wife interrupted him, "It's all right." she looked at him with daggers.

"Would you like me to use a calculator, sir?" I asked.

His wife, again going red, said, "No it's all right."

"Yes," he replied, so I went to get the calculator. As I was walking away I heard her having a right go at him. So I did it on the machine – I had my toes, legs and fingers crossed – please let it be right, I was saying to myself. It came out to the penny, exactly as I had worked it out. I kept showing him the calculator, and his wife kept apologizing; he didn't care, he was happy to know he hadn't been fiddled. I helped them load up the van, I never got a tip, and as they got into their van she was still having a go at him. Next customer here I come.

At the end of that day the boss came up to me and pushed a five-pound note into my top pocket. "Thanks, Dave, you did a great job today, you are the best salesman I've ever had."

The manager said, "What does he think the rest of us have been doing, sitting on our backsides?"

All the other staff were annoyed. It was a bad move on his part, because they all said, "Right, we won't try anymore." They were the sales team; I was only the delivery driver.

The only trouble with selling a lot of bathroom suites on a Saturday was it meant a lot of deliveries in the week. Come Monday morning we loaded the van only to find I had two deliveries in Hall Green and a delivery in Stechford and one in Chelmsley Wood. Trouble was, they were all for dinnertime, twelve noon. Of course I got it in the neck from all the customers, I was late getting to them. I think the sales team were getting their own back and all because the boss gave me a fiver in front of them. When I got back I asked them why they put the delivery times at the same time, and with a smile they said, "Oh dear, you shouldn't have sold so many, should you?" as they walked away from me. That fiver gave me a very hard time and the boss lost sales because of it.

After that I went into the shower room selling the showers on a Saturday; that was an interesting job. All the sales were down and the boss never knew why. They all gave up trying, mind you, it made my job easier – a lot less deliveries, more time to myself. I got fed up, the sales staff weren't happy, and the customers were moaning.

One Wednesday afternoon when I was serving, the boss said, "Dave, the till was down yesterday, so will you not go on it anymore; leave all the money side to Derrick." He always worked behind the counter selling the plumbing items. Well as you can imagine, I hit the roof and told him to, "lick em on," there and then, and I walked out. That was me back in the unemployment queue.

THE JOB I NEVER GOT

When we sold our house, number 56, Berwicks Lane, Chelmsley Wood, we moved to Warton in north Warwickshire, on the edge of the countryside, number 102-104 Orton Road. I had been working for a company called D and G Supplies; this company sold bathroom suites, plumbing equipment, kitchen suites and tools. With the new house being 17 miles from work, I of course handed in my notice, yes jobless once again.

For the first time in our lives we received from our solicitor a cheque for £2,000. We were advised to apply for a grant from the council to renovate the cottages we had just bought. The council approved a grant of £2,000, but only as the work progressed. In the meantime I found a warehouse that sold cane and basket ware, you know the type, raffia and dried grasses, it was all the rage at the time so I bought mountains of it, so much I couldn't get it all in the car. It was very cheap, so I sold it cheap. I had bought hanging baskets, hammocks, picnic baskets macramé, raffia, fly swatters, corn dollies and many, many more items of that nature. We did house parties at night.

My then wife worked as a dental nurse in Marston Green and Chelmsley Wood in Birmingham. I stayed at home ripping apart the two cottages we had just bought. I had signed on the dole, as at that time there were almost four million unemployed in the country. I used to take my wife to work in the mornings, go back home, work on the house until it was time to pick her up in the evenings, then back home I would start working again on the cottages. I knocked the two cottages into one, ripped out the ceilings in one and dug up the floors. I took out the stairs, knocked the plaster off the walls and stripped out the wiring of one house while we lived in the other one. Then repeated it all over again in the other cottage. After we had our dinner we would get changed and sell our basket ware in people's houses. To start the ball rolling I would wrap up an ornament that cost only 75p and sell strips of raffle tickets for 50p, I made as much as £10 on some occasions. I did that at every house party, sometimes I only made £3. I used to buy sand and cement, plaster and gravel with the raffle money.

Not far from our two cottages was a working coal mine and I had the idea I would become a miner – I know it's a joke, and I know it's on me! As my money was running out I needed to earn and with the lack of employment I thought I would try the coalmines. So one Monday morning on the way back from taking Irene to work, I popped into the personnel office of the coalmine to enquire about their vacancy. A round-faced little man came out to see me. "You are enquiring about the vacancy we have are you?" he asked me.

"Yes, sir." I always said sir when I was creeping to get a job.

"Where are you working at present?" he questioned.

"I'm unemployed at the moment," I told him, and his mouth opened and his eyes went wide, well that happened after I had explained I handed in my notice and left my job as the travelling was too much – it was 17 miles there and 17 miles back, 34 miles round trip and I just couldn't afford it.

"Well surely you knew that when you came to live in this area," he exclaimed.

"Well, yes I did," I explained. "I was hoping to get a job here in this village."

"And you just packed your job up – just gave it up." He started to stammer, "You, you ju... just pa... pa... packed it up so you don... don't earn any wages at... at all, just packed it up!"

I was smiling, it was then I realised no one did such things in that industry. "We have men here that... that started as very young boys, their dads and their granddads worked here, whole families, generation after generation – no one leaves, only to retire and we have to push 'em to do that. I'm sorry, son, I could not employ you." As he turned and started to walk away he was muttering to himself, "Just packed his job up." He was still muttering as he disappeared through the door. I thought it was funny; it was a normal occurrence for me to hand in my notice. So I never became a miner – that was one job I never got, to be very honest I only wanted that job so I could say "I've been a miner" as well. I might even have lasted a couple of weeks. Since then that mine has shut down. (Not because of me, I must add).

WORKING AWAY

When me and my brother John were between jobs, (I was between jobs much more than John was, he was more steadfast than I ever was) we were in our mom's back garden one afternoon when the lad who lived next door climbed up his ladders to fix his guttering. We started to have a conversation with him; his name was Stuart, he had been unemployed for a short while, and he told us he was a floor layer, well floor screeding. He was telling us he had been in touch with a firm and was waiting for the boss of the firm to tell him if he had acquired a contract that was in Wales. He asked would we be interested in working out of town, casual, cash in hand, as the job needed two labourers and a floor layer.

He did get the contract – the job was in a town named Haverfordwest in Wales, not far from St. David's. We went in my car as I was the only one with a vehicle at that time, and booked into a pub – for the life of me I can't remember the name of it, but we were on the top floor of that pub.

Next day we went to the site for a look to see what was what. It was a lovely setting. They were building an indoor market, it went about the quarter way across a river and boats were going under that building, it really was in a beautiful area. They were building walls and walkways in beautiful stone boulders, but the only drawback for me and John was to get to the top of that building with our barrow loads of floor screed. They had erected a ramp that went up a slope to a small square landing, then up another slope to a square, the same again, three slopes. Brother, that was hard work to begin with till our muscles got built up, then we enjoyed it.

We had dinner cooked for us every night, well she wasn't a cook, all we got was chips all the time, and we asked for a cooked roast dinner but never got it. Every night they had late night drinking that sometimes went on till the early hours of the morning.

One Tuesday evening we were getting ready to go for a walk around the town to see if there was a restaurant where we could get a nice meal, when we heard what seemed like a thousand women's voices. It turned out, every Tuesday was disco night, and the floor below our floor was where the ladies toilet was, and as we sat on our beds listening to the conversations of those ladies we were a little shocked I can tell you – I thought only men talked like that. Well I was a lot younger then and innocent, well younger anyway. We were away doing that job for three weeks; I loved it, happy memories.

MY SHOP

It was the one thing I wanted to do as a youngster was to have my own shop, well we all have a dream of one sort or another, but mostly we never realise our dream do we? I always fancied opening a hardware shop, I used to love the smell of them, and when seeing them on films they always looked better than they actually were in real life. As a child I was sent to the hardware shop for a ball of white and a blue, this was used to whitewash the coalhouse (yes, sounds a bit mad when I think about it now). The smell of paraffin and soaps, straw, timber, all those smells mixed together, I loved it, makes me feel very nostalgic thinking about it, and yes, I have my rose coloured glasses on as the saying goes.

I saw a shop across the road from the snooker hall I used as a youth in Stechford, the same one me and Johnny did a runner from, this shop was a very well used grocery shop in those days when I worked for Donovans, but by this time it was a second hand clothes shop. It was up for rent at twenty pounds a week. I went to the council, signed all the necessary documents and paid a month's rent in advance. The lady who had been running the shop was really glad to leave, she wanted out, but me, I was full of enthusiasm, I had this dream of a string of shops, Prossers, a string of shops all over Birmingham (well OK I can dream, can I not? It was a very short lived dream I can tell you).

I loved making models so I opened up as a hobby shop, Family Hobbies we called it (my wife begged me not to have a shop; I wish I had listened to her. I can sell and make money for anyone, but not for myself it would appear). I sold fur fabric, eyes for furry animals, matchstick kits, all sorts of things for the hobbyist, trouble was, I was still living in the forties and it was the 1980s and I thought everybody was like me, but I soon found out different; it was a disaster, it wasn't working at all.

My nephew came to see me; he had been made redundant from the Co-op where he had been a manager in the delicatessen department. "Dave, why don't you turn your shop into a delicatessen shop? If these

This photograph was taken in March 1955.
The shop on the far right became my shop in July 1979.
It was situated in Station Road, Steachford, Birmingham. At first I had it as a hobbies shop called Family Hobbies, then I changed it into a delicatessen shop called W-P Cooked Meats. It has now been demolished. The factory on the right called Parkinson Cowen made gas stoves has also been demolished.

My hobbies shop

My hobbies shop changed to a cooked meats shop, W.P. Cooked Meats hobbies ain t doing any good, I can teach you all there is to know about selling cooked meats – how to slice them up, even how to slice up half a pig and all the different cuts and how to slice up the bacon." Sounds good I thought, can't be worse than these hobbies.

So I sorted everything out with the council and the health and safety people. I bought tiles and did all the walls in tiles top to bottom, fitted in a sink, I bought fridges, scales, counters and knives, even cooler counters, all second hand from the Co-op warehouse. They stored all the fridges and counters from shops that they had closed down and I bought them for next to nothing, fifty pounds in fact. I even got scales from there at a fiver; this manager was really good to me.

My nephew Kevin, that's my sister Doreen's son, he taught me well, he knew all the right contacts to buy the meats from. I found a firm in Perry Bar called Warwick Meats, and I bought my sausages from them, 300 pounds in weight of sausage every week. We did sandwiches at dinnertime, and all the factory people would queue outside the shop for them. I ran a raffle on my first week of opening, £20 worth of free meat to one of my lucky customers for shopping at my shop. We were getting known and were doing well. We called the shop W. P. Cooked Meats. Then one Monday morning not a customer came in. Strange, I thought, OK, I will do some boning and slice up my bacon. Come dinnertime I was ready for the crowd of office workers who bought lots of sandwiches from me, but not a soul. I stood outside my shop and it was a ghost town, I just could not understand what was going on, no one had said anything to me.

On that same evening, a lady that worked in the office across the road from my shop for a haulage company, and always came into my shop, walked in. "You are my first customer today," I told her, "it's been absolutely dead, have you any idea what's going on?"

"Have you not heard, Dave? All the factories across the road there," she was pointing to factories, "have closed down and the entire workforce has been made redundant. Didn't anyone tell you last week?" she asked.

"Not a word from anyone," I told her.

That was the start of my downfall. What do I do now, I thought, I haven't recovered all of my money yet. I was thinking, OK, I will weather the storm, but it got worse and worse.

One Monday morning I opened up, filled all the counters with the cooked meats, black puddings, bacon and cheese, I made a really good display. I cleaned everywhere, I was proud of that shop, it looked good, but still no customers. After an hour I closed the shop, weighed and wrapped up all the meats in quarter, half and one pound packages, ready to go around to all my family and friends that evening and sell it all. I phoned up a company that bought second hand machines, counters and the like, told them how much I wanted, and they came the next day, took out the shop window and emptied the shop and replaced the window. I phoned the council to say I had ceased trading and was putting it up for sale. It took a few weeks to sell that shop, by which time I was in arrears – I hadn't a penny to my name. We were eating toast for Sunday lunch, I couldn't feed my two children, that hurt me the most. I sold the shop, my life's savings had gone and I had to sell my two cottages that I had worked on for three years knocking the two into one. I sold them, or should I say *it,* as it was now one dwelling and not two, and I paid off all the debts I had acquired through the shop from the sale of the cottage, and bought a cheap council house. I had cleared all my debts; I owed no one anything, and I bought the council house for cash – I had no mortgage, not a penny in the bank or in my pocket. My wife worked part time, that's how we ate, because of her, so after all that hard work at the age of forty, we were back to how we were, well we had a house.

Since then we worked hard, sold that council house, bought and sold houses and did them up as we went along. I started to collect antiques toys, which I have now sold to fund the books I have written, including this one. We now own two houses and have got a little sum of money in the bank. We are now retired and enjoying the freedom of life.

WORKING WITH BOOKS

As I was looking through the jobs that were on the boards in the job centre (known as the labour exchange) there were many, but as normal when jobs were in that place the wages offered were always very poor. As I scanned the rows of vacancies I came across what looked a very interesting job, it was a job I had never thought of doing. On the card it read: *Temporary H.G.V. driver required for six weeks only, to drive a coach converted into a mobile library.* Well I've never driven a coach, I thought to myself, nor have I ever worked with books, but I took the card to a lady sitting waiting for a fool like me to take on a low paid temporary job like this one. I was quite excited to be honest with you, I loved doing different things and seeing how things worked. I had never worked with books or driven a coach before but I really wanted the job. The lady explained to me that the regular driver was off sick, that's why the job was for such a short time. How they knew he would only be off sick for six weeks I have no idea.

I went for the interview in a little town known as Atherstone, in Warwickshire. The library wasn't a large one; I was interviewed by the Head Librarian, a very nice gentleman, very smart and quietly spoken, I bet that's because working around books they never raised their voices, well it's a thought. Any road up, after I had had the job explained to me he took me to see the vehicle, the mobile library coach. I always fancied driving a coach but you had to have a special licence called a P.S.V. (public service vehicle) for driving passengers, and as I didn't have such a licence and I only needed a class two, driving that coach really appealed to me, and I could drive it on my licence. I can now proudly say I've driven a coach. As I walked into the coach the librarian told me to sit in the driver's seat to see if I liked it. "It's OK," I said, "I don't need to sit in it, I know it's all right." But he insisted so I sat in the seat.

"How does that feel?" he enquired.

"It's fine, sir." (I always said 'sir' when I was grovelling.)

"Do you want the job?" he then asked me.

"Yes, sir," I replied.

“Good. Can you start in the morning at 9am?”

“Yes, sir.”

“Good; follow me, I will introduce you to the two ladies who you will be working with.” Now that really excited me, two ladies – I wonder if my luck will change, I was thinking to myself (I know I’m a married man, well men always hope if they are truthful). It just got better and better when I saw how beautiful the ladies were.

The next morning I got to the library an hour before my time. I was a little apprehensive because I’m not the brightest pin in the box, so I did what I always do in those circumstances, I kept quiet (I know that made a change for me) till I had some idea about what was being asked of me. As far as chatting up the ladies that was a definite no, no all they were interested in was books, oh well you can’t win them all can you? It made such a nice change to work with nice educated quietly spoken people (and they talked with a posh voice), never a word was said out of place by them, nor me if it comes to that, life for me was very pleasant at that time. I loved driving around the country lanes.

We were about half way round the route when one of the ladies left us, I think she must have been there just to make sure I was OK. The other lady told me to drive to a cottage where the driver who was off sick lived, he was doing lunch for us, he only charged five shillings – he lived on his own. His cottage was in a little village known as Wood End. I parked right outside his front gate; there was no footpath. It was a beautiful little cottage, the type I wished I lived in now in this year of 2011. As the door of the cottage opened a four foot nothing man stood there, he was as fat as two matchsticks tied together! How on earth do you drive the mobile library coach, I was thinking to myself. The inside of the cottage was a dream, I felt so at home there, low polished beamed ceilings, an inglenook fire place, polished beams surrounding it. There was an Aga cooker with a steaming kettle on it, and cast-iron saucepans simmering next to it with potatoes and vegetables in them and the smell of beef cooking (I can smell it now, and as I write I can still see the inside of that beautiful little cottage). It was winter so it was a little dark so the wall lights were on; having red shades on them they gave a very nice red glow to the white walls and the dark oak polished beams. With the flickering flames from the Aga dancing on

Delivering books all around the countryside

the ceiling for a moment I was a boy again remembering how our fire at home flickered images on the walls and ceiling. I felt so much at peace I could have been in heaven. The table and chairs were dark oak, and the table was laid with a red cloth with white plates and tureens that matched with serving ladles, and bone handled knives and forks. Yes, my friends, I was in heaven. As he opened the Aga cooker oven door there was a large earthenware dish which he pulled out and placed on the top of the Aga. He turned and said "I hope you like beef?"

"Yes," we both replied together.

"I've also made an apple pie and custard for you."

My mouth was watering as he put the veggies in the tureens and the steam came floating out; again it reminded me of home as a boy. He put the beef on a large meat dish and placed it on the table and carved it up. We handed him our plates and he was very generous with the portions; we helped ourselves to the vegetables. It was all cooked to perfection – the beef melted in one's mouth and his apple pie was to die for, as the saying goes. What a gentleman; a first class host and to top all that, a wonderful cook.

After we had eaten we chatted for half an hour. It turned out he had joined the library at the tender age of fourteen. He was called up to do his National Service in the army and he went to war for the defence of our wonderful country. He came home after being demobbed, and got his old job back at the library. I never found out why he was off sick, I never asked. He looked well to me, but looks can be deceiving, can't they? I paid him my five shillings and shook his hand. We had lunch not every day, but twice a week, and I will never forget that wonderful English gentleman, his kindness, and his wonderful cooking. His way of living is what we all dream about but never get. The first time I left that little cottage to return back to work, I turned to the young lady I worked with and said "I want that cottage and that life style."

"Me too," she replied with a smile. He was a working class man but he had all that life can offer anyone.

Off we went to rich and poor alike, cottages, manor houses, farms, I loved every moment of that job and I was very sorry when it ended. Now there was a job I would never have said "Lick em on – I'm off" to.

CLEANING UP THE ESTATE

The second time I started working for the Solihull Council I was asked if I minded cleaning toilets for a short time, a couple of weeks or so. Cleaning toilets is a job I swore I would never do – one should never say never! Well I did start to clean the toilets in the Chelmsley Wood area and I hated every second I was doing that job.

The toilets around Chelmsley Wood were vandalised on a daily basis. I was asked by the foreman if I would nail up the doors of the cubicles on one particular toilet block because the pans had been smashed and were dangerous to the public, as china when broken is extremely sharp. So with lengths of timber, six feet long by three inches wide by one inch thick, and six inch nails, I nailed up all the doors to each cubicle from the inside. I climbed back over the partitions (I was fit in those days) and assumed that all would be OK from there on in. The next morning, to my surprise, the lads from that estate had worked very hard to open those doors, they had kicked and bashed them till they could no longer be called doors, they were in pieces. The noise they made must have been immense; why the neighbours living close by never did anything about it I will never understand. I went straight back to the depot and made out my report. A team went out and locked up the toilet block, and it was never used again, so the older folk of that area had a long walk to the town centre if they needed to use a toilet. That toilet block has since been demolished. I hope those mindless idiots when they become elderly, find when they are taken short that the toilets they wish to use are closed down or have been demolished.

I was taken off the toilets (I'm glad to say) and given a little tipper van to drive. My new job was going all around the Chelmsley Wood Estate emptying the concrete rubbish bins at the end of every walk way. They were all full of garden rubbish, and as soon as I emptied them they were filled up by the next morning. One morning as I was removing clods of turf, house bricks, boulders, metal objects, from one of those bins, a gentleman came out of his house and said, " These bins cause more trouble than they are worth, if they weren't here I'm sure the area would be cleaner." So I told my foreman what had been said.

"OK, Dave," he replied, "go to the stores and get a sledge hammer and start to knock them all down, but I haven't told you to do it, you will have to say you know nothing about it."

So back to the bins I went and over a couple of weeks I demolished dozens of them – no one from the council ever noticed that they no longer existed.

I went around that area for a few weeks and it was always clean, which meant I was having a really easy job, I was getting paid for doing nothing. When the foreman finally realised I was doing nothing, he put me driving the gully emptying lorry (that's the drains in the road). Those drain covers were very heavy, mind you I was quite strong in my youth. They were hard to move at times because of the traffic running over them all the time, and with the dirt going down the sides of them they became wedged. So with a sledge hammer I hit one corner of the drain cover and that always worked, it made it loose so I could then lift it off to suck all the rubbish out with the long vacuum hose into the tank on the back of the lorry.

In between driving the gully emptier, I drove a little lorry; I used that lorry like it was my own. For two weeks I went to my brother's house that he had just purchased, and I worked pulling down the ceilings. I filled the lorry up every day with the rubbish from those ceilings and took it to the tip. When the foreman asked where I had been working I told him the name of a road, and he would say, I looked for you there, I would then say, well after that I went to such a road, and he would reply, I went there as well, we must have been passing each other all the time. I got away with it for weeks. I was moving rubbish for myself and for my friends all the time; it's no wonder the council struggle for money, for I was not alone doing my own thing in work's time. I liked that job but the jobs one liked doing were always low pay.

One morning the boss was in a bad mood and he started to have a go at me, so, yes, my favourite saying was used, lick em on – I'm off.

S. G. B.

Scaffolding, Great Britain – this firm is based next to Birmingham airport. I got the job from the job centre in Chelmsley Wood; it was only temporary, eight weeks in total, not a bad job.

I worked in a shed with no doors; my job was to sand down the shuttering boards that had been returned from the building sites all around the country. Any holes and deep scratches had to be filled in with car body filler; I think it was called Tetrasill. Mixing the paste with the hardener, which came in small tubes, it went hard in seconds, then with an electric drill gun with a sanding disc fitted in the chuck, the whole board was sanded till all the concrete and body filler was smooth, then the boards were put in piles awaiting the fork lift to take them into the yard. They were then put on top of many other boards ready for the next building site that would be concreting new walls. When the walls were finished those shuttering boards were returned to the S. G. B. yard where I worked, and the sanding process started all over again. The boss liked the way I worked and said I was a hard worker and would I like a permanent job with a rise in pay. I refused; I wanted to try to get a job I had never done before. I had no staying power at all, so I left and was again unemployed and I signed on the dole. The only excuse I can give in my defence is once I had mastered a job, I got bored, the challenge had gone – maybe I was lazy as well. When in a new job, I loved the challenge of mastering it. What's that I hear you say? I was irresponsible? I was, and that's the truth.

SECURITY GUARD

I worked a few times as a security guard, but I wasn't keen on this job, it was the kind of a job not many people liked doing. It was always cash in hand, and I worked sometimes in department stores. The young lads I found to be the worst, always trying to prove themselves, especially when they were with young girls – some of the shops deserved to get robbed. I know it's wrong to steal, but when you don't know where your next meal is coming from it makes one change from the way one normally acts. I know, I've been down and out; OK, I had a house, but no food or money, nothing coming in, and no one to turn to. Yes, I've been there. I might add it was all my own doing.

I worked nights in London in the Next shops. Their stores were having all the floors sanded and resealed; all the doors had to be open as the fumes from the sealant were overpowering. The finish was superb. I caught one of the workers going through the shoes; he soon stopped when he saw me. Mind you, me a security guard, that's a joke, while the floor sealant was drying we all got our heads down. I went fast asleep and one of the workers had a hard time waking me up. He remarked, "Boy, when you sleep you die, I had a real job waking you up!" They could have stolen lots of items, I'm sure they did. Did I care? No, not at all. I was getting two pounds fifty pence an hour cash in hand, no tax; slave labour wages, so I was only there for the money.

After all the Next shops had been done, I was sent to a place called Corby, Northamptonshire to a Woolworth store. The youths there were bad; it seemed nearly all of them there were banned from that store, the girls as well as the boys. They tested me all day long. I escorted many of them out of the store. They would try to see how weak I was; when I grabbed one of them by the arm he soon realised he was no match for me, so he stood outside the store shouting abuse at me, showing off in front of his mates and the girls – I think he was hiding his embarrassment at being thrown out of the store.

The manageress came up to me one day and said, "Watch that man there." She pointed to a man that looked ok to me; shows you can never tell. "He carries a knife and he steals." So I made sure he was aware of me. I did see him put a cassette tape in his pocket and then walk out of the store and I let him, I wasn't about to get stabbed for two pounds fifty pence an hour, well for any amount of money if it comes to that.

A woman came up to me and introduced herself as the store detective – her nose looked like she had been ten rounds with a heavyweight boxer. She told me her nose had been punched so many times over the years, that's why it looked like it did. I asked why she did such a job, and with a surprised look, said, "I love this work, don't you?"

I very quickly replied, "No." I was just filling in, I normally worked nights in the security game. I'm a peaceful loving fella, and I like the countryside. Chasing thieves and throwing people out of places is not me, I told her. I'm only here for the money; store security was a big no no for me. That Woolworths was the last store I worked in as a security guard. New horizons here I come.

GOVERNMENT SCHEME

This was the first government scheme I went on. I was working in peoples' gardens in the Atherstone area of Warwickshire; I worked two days one week and three the next week. I don't think I had a title, I did all sorts of jobs from digging over gardens, hedge cutting, sweeping up grass, seeding, even taking up lawns from the front of a house and relaying it in the back garden. The idea was to help the senior citizens that couldn't do the gardens themselves. We started to do young ladies gardens, and when I questioned them about this I was told to mind my own business. Just as I thought; the charge hand was taking back-handers, and not sharing it with us, his four workers, so I refused to do any gardens unless they were senior citizens.

As the weeks passed and the winter set in and the days became frost bitten, I asked the management if we were going to get a shanty to have our lunch in. "No," was the reply, "go to the nearest pub."

"That's not possible," I explained, "we are doing gardens in the country lanes at isolated cottages and there isn't a pub for miles. The foreman goes home in his car for dinner, so we are stranded." (It was agreed that any foreman taking on the job would use his car to transport the workforce to and from the job wherever it may be.) On one occasion we had to sit in a greenhouse, the wind was howling, everywhere was white with frost. It was colder inside that greenhouse than it was outside of it, so we sat at the back of the greenhouse outside to shelter from the wind to eat our lunch. Two of us went to the office to complain about the conditions, and we were told to get on with it and to stop complaining. We invited the two persons working in the office to join us for lunch in the greenhouse; of course they refused and accused us of being moaners, as they sat in their very hot office.

So they transferred me to the Coleshill group of gardeners. I was close to home with that group, and I had my car then on the road, funny thing was I never went home. The foreman was a much nicer person than the one on the other scheme, his name was Les, and we had a laugh with him. We did more playing around than we did gardening, mind you, when we did a garden it looked really good when we had finished it. I even as a favour to the foreman plumbed a tap in his outside garden toilet for him.

They gave them the title of foreman but like us they were just labourers. He was full time but only for a twelve month period. I did my two days one week and three the other, and at the end of the twelve months I was back on the dole. When those schemes finished, all that were employed went back on the dole. One thing I did notice among the youth that worked on those schemes was that it was soul destroying for them; they felt useless when thrown back on the unemployment system. Me I did OK, I knew how to survive one way or the other.

B.V.S.C

This was a firm, well a scheme, which was started up in the 1980s by the government in the depression; it was a way for the government to get young people working. It was a scheme where the young generation of the country worked two days one week and three the next. What the job was really, was to clean up the country. These jobs were advertised in the job centres as trainee gardeners, if you can call cleaning a waste piece of ground up on street corners and erecting a little wooden barrier up and raking over the soil without weeding, then throwing grass seed over it, gardening. OK – they were training as gardeners. All the lads moaned all the time saying, "We are just labouring, we wanted to be trained as gardeners."

We worked in the Aston Cross, Lozells, Perry Barr, Selly Oak, Small Heath, Tyseley, Acocks Green, and Handsworth, and my job was driving a lorry. I had two lads to do the labouring for me, there was about one hundred and fifty youngsters working there, they were in groups of eight plus the driver who had the privilege of being called the charge hand. The vehicle was a thirty-five hundred weight van. The youths had to sit on the wooden boxes along both sides of the van, that's where all the tools were kept and I might add padlocked up – there were a few vans. I was full time but the scheme only allowed me twelve months employment, then back on the dole. My job was to drive around to all the different sites where the teams were and load any rubbish they had accumulated, throw it into the lorry then off to the tip. I soon found out how unfair that job was. On some jobs where there was a load of earth that had been cleared from a site and left in a big pile by a team of eight or ten youths, it was expected that my two lads would load it on to the lorry. I soon put a stop to that. I used to get the team plus my two lads in a line and told them to do two shovelfuls each, that way my two lads were not worked to death, as the saying goes. On a good note, those two lads loved working with me; I would take them home early and clock them out or drop them off in the middle of town. I treated that lorry like it was my own and the job likewise. I would go joyriding in it round the country lanes, and use it to do jobs that were nothing to do with the firm, and get paid. I gave the lads any money we earned from the jobs we did – I always shared it out equally between them, well they were poorly paid so any extra was a Godsend to them.

Every morning was a trip to a café before we started work. Every Monday morning I used to go to the Birmingham rag market, and there was always an antiques fair on. I used to park outside the market, leave the two lads in the lorry and tell them to say I was inside looking for a Mr Jones, I had to pick up some rubbish, just in case a traffic warden tried to book me for illegal parking. I got away with that for a whole twelve months! That was my last job, the end of my working life – I hurt my neck and back, and became riddled with arthritis. I hated work anyway.

STUBBINS

I worked on Stubbins sites, but I didn't work for Stubbins direct, I worked for a carpenter, cash in hand. The site agent asked the carpenter why I always turned up at nine and not eight like he did; he told him I had to take my little boy to school. The agent thought I was a carpenter.

I was working on a roof one day fixing the rafters, and as I turned round I noticed the site agent was watching me, he never said a word, he was satisfied I was a carpenter and never bothered me again. Me a carpenter, that's a laugh! I'm what's known in the trade as a butcher of wood, mind you I have seen carpenters that weren't as good as me and I'm no good. I did it all with that carpenter, first and second fix, first fix being joists, roof timbers etc. and second fix being architrave, skirting boards and doors etc, on those houses. Stubbins paid the best wages of all the well-known builders. That company no longer exists, they went broke, and no – it wasn't because of me! Well it might have been – most of the places I worked for or at have ceased trading or their premises have been demolished.

APPENDICES

ROOMS AND HOUSES

I was born two years before the end of World War II, in October 1943. I was born and grew up at 38, Plowden Road, Glebe Farm, Stechford, Birmingham 33, and that's where I lived till I was eighteen.

My friends and I used to go to the pictures (cinema) every Saturday evening to find a tart, that's what we called young girls in those days; nowadays the lads call them birds, even totty. The picture houses we used in the forties and fifties were the Atlas, Beaufort and the Capital. There was a place, or should I say area, not far from where I lived called Shard End, next to an area known as Castle Bromwich, and there was a picture house there called the Castle Cinema. One Saturday morning my friend Trevor Kendall told me Cliff Richard was showing at the Castle Cinema – the film was called *Espresso Bongo*, so for the first time in my life I went to the Castle Cinema that evening, not to see the film but to see if I could get a tart. We had no luck that Saturday evening. "Well, that was a waste of time," I said to Trevor.

"It's OK, Dave, we can try next week."

"Yeah, that's true, Trev," I replied. So we decided to go to that cinema the next Sunday evening to find a couple of tarts.

We did what we did in every cinema we visited, we walked up and down the aisles trying to see if there were any girls sitting on their own, all the boys did that in those days, looking and hoping to find the girl of their dreams. Just to have a girl talk to me would have made me very happy, girls didn't go for me in those days. We changed our minds and went to the Atlas cinema on the Saturday evening; we went to the Castle Cinema on the Sunday evening instead. Any road up, as we were walking up and down the aisles, Trevor caught hold of my arm. "In here, Dave, there's a couple of tarts."

I looked but I could see only darkness so we sat down. When my eyes came used to the dark, I noticed a couple of girls sitting in front of us. "Trev, Trev," I said shaking his arm, "girls in front."

"I know," he said, "why do you think I said sit here?"

The film showing was *The Last of the Hunt*. That evening was to change the rest of my life; a whole new way of life lay ahead for me. Trevor being Trevor started to touch the girls' hair, they turned and smiled at him. The girl in front of me had a duffle coat, charcoal grey with white fur lining. Trevor said, "Look at her coat, Dave, they ain't half expensive."

The girl turned and said something to Trevor, I can't remember what now, but I made a comment and stroked her hair. I was shaking, waiting for the normal response of being told to get lost, but that never happened so I started to run my fingers up and down her face. To my unexpected surprise she allowed it! I was, to say the least, very excited. Trevor and another friend were chatting up her friend. I got really daring; I leant over her seat and kissed her, and I knew at that very moment what the opposite sex did for a man's insides, or at that time boy's – what boys say to impress the girls and our actions, are at the very least bizarre. As we walked the girls home my two mates were, how can I put it? – when birds dance and show their feathers, and Rhinos show their strength – my two mates were doing just that. Brother, did they look and sound stupid, and it was at that very moment I realised just how pathetic I had been in the past when trying to impress the opposite sex. It's something boys have to do as they are growing up; girls never seem to have to do such silly things. I smile now when I see and hear the young lads trying to impress the young girls, mind you when it works there isn't a feeling in the world like it! I was locked in the arms of the girl that bowled me over while Trevor and Michael were still trying to impress Susan Godden. The girl I was kissing was Irene Parker; she wore white slip-on shoes with a big white button in the middle of them, the skirt and top were lilac and white check that she had made herself, and with the duffle coat she looked to me a million dollars, and she was.

I was wearing (and I thought I looked great) black slip-on shoes, white socks, black trousers, orange shirt, light green jumper with an orange v neck, and a grey coat with black and white dots; the white was mixed in with the black dots, not separate, with locks over the pockets, I say locks, they were pieces of material with a buttonhole at the bottom of them and they buttoned up over the pocket. I had bought all my clothes on HP (hire purchase) a couple of weeks before. I must have looked like a clown. I met Irene inside the Castle cinema at approx 7.45pm on the thirteenth of March, 1960 (poor girl). We got married at All Saints Church, Shard End, Birmingham, because where your young lady lived that's where you had to get married. On the evening of our wedding day, we slept on a mattress on the floor of Irene's parents' living room; I smoked at that time. The day I got married, I hadn't a cigarette, not a penny piece to my name, no bank account, no nothing, I suppose really we should not have got married but she was three months pregnant. Irene had five shillings – that was our wealth. Well, we had each other and that's all that mattered at that moment in time, so apart from five shillings we had nothing.

When I met Irene on the 13th of March 1960, she worked at Barrows stores in the Birmingham city centre as a wages clerk, and I worked as a rounds boy for the CO-OP bakery Manor Road in Stechford, Birmingham. The day we got married Irene worked for a firm called Donovans, who I used to work for but I left. I used to play for Donovans' football team; we won the league that year. My new job was at Kunzles. Donovans made electric interiors for mains electric cabinets to go in factories or very large buildings, Kunzles made cakes.

Our lives changed as they do when one gets married. The day before I got married I moved all my belongings from my mom's house to Irene's parents' house; I had a bike that I had bought out of my paper round money and three Kunzles paper carrier bags, yes all my worldly possessions were in three Kunzles paper carrier bags, but I was very happy. As Irene became more pregnant she left Donovans and worked part time for a lady who ran a sweet shop just up the road from where we lived, the shop was called Keens. We only stayed at Irene's parents' home for a short time, trouble was I was really common and her dad couldn't stand the sight of me, he would have done anything to have got me away from Irene. Looking back now at the young me, if my daughter had met someone like me, I too would have worried like Irene's dad did.

Irene's parents lived at 132, Timberley Lane, Shard End. My first son was born there in 1962, we named him Anthony. Just before he was born I papered and painted the bedroom so it looked nice for my wife and when all her family and friends called to see her with our new son. The trouble was there were stripes in the paper and I got them slightly on the slope, everyone thought it was great but I think people were just being kind. The paper was white with tiny lilac flowers, the doors were lilac and the paintwork white. I was very proud of my first painting and decorating job, Irene said she loved it and was very proud of me (I wonder if she would say that nowadays, yeah, I think she would).

In July 1962, as I could not get on with Irene's dad, we found rooms in a big old house in Birmingham, an area known as Erdington. The house was in Mason road, I think it was number 2; it had been turned into flats. It was quite run down but we moved in. In July 1962, the rent was £2/15/-0d a week. We took the flat on the second floor, it had two more flats up in the attic, and we lived there for only four weeks. After the first week I walked into the house from work, and as I started to climb the stairs my wife popped her head out from the flat on the ground floor. She told me the landlord had asked if we would move to the ground floor flat, as we had a young baby and it would be easier to get the pram in and out of the house, plus it was a nice view out of the French windows onto the garden. The interior was worn and dirty, and as my son was only six weeks old then I was concerned for his health. One evening as I was plugging in the iron, into the light socket, the light fitting fell off and left the bare wires hanging from the ceiling. On closer examination I found the fitting was held in by matchsticks! Just thinking about that now makes me angry; that was a very dangerous thing to do – and my son at times in his pram would have been asleep under that light fitting!

One Saturday afternoon a young lady appeared with a man and a baby; it turned out she had left her husband and was outcast by her family as she had had an affair, got pregnant and bought shame on the family. She was a twin and came from a wealthy family. We helped her and gave her things as she had nothing. We ourselves had only one knife and fork each and two spoons, even our baby clothes were hand me downs. We tried hard to clean up the place but it was a job too far at that time, so my wife, Irene, asked her dad if we could go back to his house for a short time. The rent on the flat was paid up to date, but the landlord said we had to give two weeks' notice and find him another tenant, so Irene's dad came late afternoon to move us out, but the tenant in the other flat was a friend of the landlord's and she phoned and told him we were moving out. He didn't live far away because he came around to see us before we had got everything in the car, and what we had would have hardly filled a car boot. Well the landlord was red-faced and very angry shouting and waving his arms about. "You are not leaving," he shouted, and then he grabbed the father-in-law's suitcase that we had just filled, saying, "Well, I'm going to have this," and he ran out of the door and attempted to go up the stairs. My father-in-law chased after him, caught hold of the suitcase, and as he did the handle broke.

"That's it now," Irene's dad said to him, "I will sue you for damages."

"You are not leaving," the landlord kept shouting, so I slipped out and called the police. When the police arrived they tried in vain to calm down the landlord, but it was hopeless, he kept saying, "My brother is a policeman."

"Where is he?" he was asked time and again. After the police officer had asked a few more times, the landlord said, "In Dublin, Ireland."

"That's it," the police officer said, as he shoved him out into the hallway and into the kitchen, "now stay away from these people and let them leave."

Irene got into the car with my son Anthony. I only had two suitcases left to put into the car, so her dad started the engine. I ran as fast as I could with the suitcases, threw them into the boot of the car, and we newlyweds were driven away from what then was a terrifying ordeal. Welcome to the world of married life, I thought. Even though Irene's dad didn't like me, he was there to help his daughter as any good father should be.

Back at Irene's parents' house once more in Timberly Lane, we had the little small bedroom that my son Anthony was born in, the one I had decorated. We were there for only three weeks when Irene found rooms in a house in Shard End, not far from her parents house, this house was in Priestland Road. I moved all our belongings on a pram, mind you all we had was a cot, a borrowed suit case and a few clothes, and in just over half an hour we had moved.

We set up the bedroom and left some bags in the dining room. We had rented the dining room and the bedroom and shared the kitchen, but it was never going to work, the woman only wanted the money, she never wanted us there at all, she lived on her own with her little dog and her tins of snuff.

After the first night, she said, "Would you move all that rubbish out of the dining room?" I explained it wasn't rubbish, it was our clothes and we had rented the dining room. She was a very funny little lady, we laughed because every night she took her little dog to bed, and her tin of snuff. The house smelt of snuff, we only stayed there for three weeks; we couldn't stand it any longer; that was September1962.

I went and asked my mom if we could live with her. "I will ask your father," she said; she always said that, even if he said no, mom would say yes, dad had no say in the matter; he wouldn't go against my mom. Any road up, we moved again. I moved all our belongings on our pram, as many people did in those days, it was not unusual to see those type of happenings. It felt really good to be back home, and everything went well for a while – of course my mom always let Irene know whose house it was, dad on the other hand didn't care so long as his meals were on the table. He was never keen on the nappies hanging all around the fireguard and hanging in the kitchen, mind you he never moaned much about it – to be honest, I hated to see those nappies everywhere, never mind my dad. It was good for me living at home, but not so good for Irene.

One evening in December 1962, Irene told me her dad had agreed to let us stay with them at their new semi-detached house, so we left my mom's house again, on our pram. Their new house was in West Avenue, Castle Bromwich, and at that time that area came under the Meriden County Council, Warwickshire. I thought, what a posh house; it had a long back garden and a proper shed – I refurbished a baby walker in that shed, it felt really good, when I was in there it was my den. I thought, I'm going to get a shed when I get a house of my own (I know what you are thinking, and you are right), it was however many years later before I lived that dream. Living with Irene's parents for the second time did not improve from the first time, well not for me anyway.

Trevor Kendall and his wife Patricia came to visit us one afternoon, and I did what all good mannered Brummies do, I asked them if they would like a cup of tea, so I went into the kitchen and put the kettle on. Irene's dad walked in and asked me "What do you think you are doing?" I explained that our friends had come to see us and I was making a cup of tea for them. "Oh no you are not," he replied, and turned off the kettle. Going back in to see my friends and telling them I couldn't give them a cup of tea was I think the most embarrassing thing I have ever done in my life; Irene was more embarrassed than I was because it was her parents' home. I was never accepted by Irene's dad, he spoke to me only when and if he had to.

Some weekends I would help my eldest brother Donald, he had a car repair shed in Orphanage road, Erdington. I was trying to learn as much as I could about cars. It was a fruitful exercise; it helped me a great deal in later years of my life.

When it became more difficult to live with Irene's parents we moved. Irene found more rooms for us to look at, they were in the Strechford area of Birmingham, in Fredrick road, right by Stechford railway station – that was in February 1963. I loved that station, and the house backed on to the railway lines. Again it was a big old Victorian house that had been turned into flats, it was just like all the others we had looked at, run down and dirty, but still it was ours and we would be on our own. We had a sitting room on the second floor and a bedroom in the attic. In the attic newspaper was pushed in the cracks all around the window, it was a sash window, and on very hot days that bedroom was airless, we couldn't sleep, it was unbearable. In our living room we had a sink and it started to leak. I knew nothing in those days about plumbing, so we put bowls under the leak but as it got worse it filled the bowl much quicker than was good for the couple down below. We shared the kitchen which was on the same landing as our living room; originally it would have been the small bedroom. The stop tap was under the sink in the kitchen, this turned off all the water to the whole of the second floor. I explained to the couple on our floor about the leak and would they be kind enough to turn off the stopcock whenever they used the kitchen sink, but not once did they turn off that stopcock, I asked them many times but they just didn't care. I never can understand why people are so horrible; I always go out of my way to help people. Irene is a gentle soul and always helped anyone that needed help, it really hurt her when the couple did what they did, or really what they didn't do. We never knew what to expect when we got back to the flat, it must have ruined the ceiling of the flat down below us, the landlady just didn't seem to care, and it took over a week to have that leak fixed.

There was a Scottish older lady a lovely jovial person in a bedsit, and in other rooms a very friendly couple who were really nice living downstairs, and between us all we tidied up the back garden and cut the hedge to have a nice place to sit and chat. Many of those types of houses in the 1960s were turned into flats and they were always dirty looking. We did our best to clean them up when we had them but they needed more than a lick of paint. We left those premises in October 1963, and went back to live at my mom's at 38 Plowden Road, as my sister had just got married and mom had a spare room. It was nice for me to be back home again, me being a typical mommy's boy, that's what Irene kept telling me.

Any road up, we stripped that bedroom's wallpaper, we laid new lino that we purchased from Stanley James, that was our local hardware shop, we papered and painted – a yellow paper with little flowers on it with blue stripes, the woodwork was blue doors, with white skirting and window frames and architrave. I fixed a broom stale across the recess, wall to wall, and hung a green plastic curtain and used it as a wardrobe, it was great, I could now hang my one and only coat up instead of hanging it on the bedroom door. There wasn't any bedroom furniture in my mom's house, just a bed, well mom had a wardrobe, no rugs or carpets anywhere in those bedrooms, but mom did have a peg rug that she had made out of old coats in the living room, it felt very nice to sit on when there was a fire.

Irene had a little trouble with my mom, she tried very hard to please her but alas, Mom didn't allow it to work – understandable I suppose two females in the same kitchen, that's a non starter. Mother and daughter no problem, daughter-in-law, now that's a different ball game. One evening Irene put a saucepan of potatoes on the gas stove ready for my tea when I got home from work; my mom had taken the saucepan off the stove and put her saucepan on but never told Irene. Well that really upset Irene. As I walked into the kitchen via the back door Irene with tears in her eyes said, "I'm ever so sorry, Dave, your tea will be late tonight."

"That's alright," I told her after she had explained what my mom had done.

One day my mom even said to Irene that our son Anthony was hers. My sister Doreen said, "My God, Mother, she did give birth to him!" Mom must have thought me being her son, my son was hers as well. Well time passed, it was forgotten, well, put to one side anyway.

One Sunday evening, Dad was sitting at the table, so was Mom, Irene was sitting by the fire, and I was sitting on the other side, when Anthony came running up to me all excited with a small piece bread in his hand. I thought he had picked it up off the floor, I took it off him and said, "It's dirty, son," and threw it in the fire. Well Anthony cried his little heart out. My dad swore at me and called me all sorts of names and Mom shouted at me; it turned out my dad had given that piece of bread to Anthony. I tried to explain I thought he had picked it from off the floor, but they said I was lying, I was just being spiteful. Irene picked up Anthony and ran upstairs (if I could change anything in my life it would be those few seconds, it hurts me just thinking about that time). The next morning my mom told me she wanted us out of the house that day, we were no longer wanted there, and all over a little mistake – that was on the 13th of June 1964.

Irene had a friend named Brenda Benbow that she went to school with. We had been invited to tea there as Irene's parents now lived in Wales, and as it was Irene's 21st birthday Brenda's mom thought it would be nice for Irene. Brenda still lived at home with her parents; they lived in Hall Hayes Road, Shard End, Birmingham. Brenda's mom could see how upset Irene was so she insisted on us staying the night at her house; we slept on the bed settee in the living room.

The next morning we went to the council office in Broad Street, Birmingham city centre, to declare ourselves homeless. They put Irene and the baby in a home for homeless mothers, and they told me to go and fend for myself. I have no recollection where I stayed that night, none at all.

Irene's nanny Parker had a friend named Tom who had a house in Ward End in Sladefield Road, at the back of the Capital picture house. He said we could stay at his house but only for four weeks because Irene's cousin Diane had been promised the rooms and Diane and her husband to be were getting married in four weeks time. Irene worked hard at finding us rooms, she found rooms in Highfield Road, Alum Rock, Saltley (that's the area my mom was born in, she came from Ash road); that was in August 1964. Again we had the rooms on the second floor. Irene and her friend Carol scrubbed that flat top to bottom and I decorated it, again blue and white, my favourite colours. Irene worked part time with Carol at a post office in Bordesley Green, next to East Birmingham Hospital, it now known as Heartlands, when my mom used to take me there it was called little Bromwich. My mom never called that hospital by any other name, it was always Little Bromwich.

My son Anthony had a scooter for Christmas. As Irene turned her back for a few seconds Anthony had followed her into the kitchen on his scooter. He fell, put out his arm as one does, but there was a three inch gap between the kitchen units and the flex of the electric kettle was always hung down inside that gap. Anthony's arm went down the gap and he caught the flex and tipped over the kettle which had just boiled, (this is heart breaking to write) and it took the skin off his face, neck and shoulder. I was outside at the time trying to get my van started, but when I got back to the flat I was given the news about my son. I'm going to leave it there – I just can't face thinking about it anymore. We left that flat; again we had trouble with the landlord;

he wanted two weeks rent in advance and for us to find a new tenant for him or we couldn't leave – that was February 1965. My eldest brother Donald said we could have one of his flats; he had converted a shop into flats and built a car repair garage at the rear, that was in Booth Street, Handsworth, so with his van he came to move us out of Highfield Road. The lady that had rented the ground floor flat left a few days before we intended to move. Any road up, on the evening we intended to move out the landlord started to work on the ground floor flat, so I phoned my brother from a phone box and explained about the landlord and for him to come late. The landlord worked till nine thirty, so we did a very late night move – our rent was paid up so we weren't doing anything wrong. The landlords in those days, from what I experienced, were horrible, well to me and mine they were anyway, and we always played the game, so at my brother's flat we felt secure. We had the ground floor living room, the bedroom was upstairs where there were two flats, and the trouble was our bedroom was next to the toilet. We had to share it with two other couples, but they were nice people.

My daughter Wendy was born in that bedroom on the 5th of August 1965, I was there at the birth, what a wonderful moment! She was born with ginger hair and the midwife said, "Ginger hair, you have some explaining to do young lady." I was a very jealous man in those days, that comment could have caused very serious problems as my wife and I had brown hair. The midwife couldn't understand the change in the hair. My sister's two children had ginger hair, and both parents had brown hair, also Irene's great aunt had ginger hair and other cousins, so I wasn't surprised my daughter had ginger hair.

I did that flat up; I even separated the kitchen from the living room with a partition wall, which I got paid for by my brother. One nice day we were offered a council house in Downing Street, number 78, just off Booth Street, it was about three hundred yards away from my brother's flats. It was a one up and one down with a kitchen that was four feet wide, and six feet long, with a Belfast sink and one cold water tap. It was a one up, but the council put up a partition across the bedroom with a door that opened straight onto the stairs, but being so dangerous we never used that room. The living room had a fire grate, very small, it was a grey tiled fireplace, and a door shut off the stairs. The toilets were in the middle of a field which was supposed to be the gardens, and there were three toilets in a block shared by all the tenants, six couples and their children in all; it was a newly built block of toilets. The reason the toilets were in a field was all the back houses had been knocked down, our row of terraced houses all six were on the front facing the road with an entry in the middle of the block, and we were on the end of the block. There were houses joined to our house at one time, but they had been demolished, so from our house to the pub on the corner known as the Phoenix, it was now a field, well, overgrown land where once stood houses. We were happy; Wendy was two months old and Anthony was three by this time. It was our first rent book; we were told we would be there for only six months as there was a demolition order on the houses, but it was two years and six months in all.

I made a garden and planted it up; I put up a little fence with a path up the middle. We loved our little house, and I decorated it top to bottom – all the other tenants said we were barmy as the houses were being demolished; why bother? "It's our home," I told them, "we love our little home." All those tenants had been there for a long time. We had a rent man call every week for the rent in those days, 15/- fifteen shillings, the boundary changed from Birmingham to Smethwick and our rent went down to fourteen and ten pence, 14/10d.

The rent man said, "It's nice to see a person take pride in where they live, so I'm going to help you get a house."

He got us a house in Chelmsley Wood, Birmingham (that move changed our lives forever, thanks to that rent man, and all because we had pride in where we lived). The day we were moving the neighbours came out saying, "How come you have got a house and you were last in this block?"

I just said, "I don't know. They were angry. That was in January 1968.

We walked in to our new home and it was heaven. We hadn't much furniture, and no carpets – the house looked empty, but it was ours now

My wife Irene in 1966, standing in a field that was once an area of back-to-back council houses. Just to the right of her is a block of three toilets; these were also in the middle of the field. One of those toilets was ours, we shared it with the family next door to us – not nice having to use the toilet in the middle of the night, or when it rained, and even worse when it snowed having to walk through the wet grass.

Our house was in a block of six that was on the front. Our front door opened onto the pavement. Those six were the last ones standing. There was an entrance in the middle of our block that gave us access to our back doors. It used to also be the access for the back houses that had been demolished. We were told our block was to be demolished in six months, that's why we took it.

We were living there for two and a half years. It was a one up and one down house. We had two small children at that time. It was our first council house, our first rent book.

to build a new life for my family. The house had been decorated and painted throughout, it had a modern kitchen, and would you believe it a box of twelve, thirteen amp plugs given free with every house. Then the milkman, Midland Counties, said if we took them on as our milkman we would receive six egg cups free – we were in shock, all this was now ours, we were so grateful and we took nothing for granted. And to top all that we had central heating. We were happy, very happy, we came from slums at 14/10d a week fourteen shillings and ten pence, now we had a brand new palace at £5-1-0 a week, five pounds one shilling. That house was in Brickhill Drive, and we lived there from January 1968 to December 1968.

We asked the rent man if we could move to an end house on the edge of the estate with a bigger garden, as we had been good tenants. We were offered a house in Berwicks Lane, still on the Chelmsley Wood Estate, number 56; it was still being built when we first saw it, we couldn't believe our luck, a double fronted house. The back garden was very private; it had the gable end of a house at the end of the garden so we weren't overlooked. At the side of the house was a wide piece of ground that had been planted with bushes so that made our garden even more private. We moved into that house on the 14th of December 1968. I was happy; I had my wonderful wife Irene, and my wonderful two children Anthony and Wendy. Irene worked really hard for her family (and still does). We decorated that house top to bottom. After we had been there quiet awhile, as just like the house in Brickhill drive it had been papered and painted throughout. I landscaped the garden back and front with my wife Irene; she could turn her hand to anything, she even made me a suit one day to go to a wedding as I hadn't any decent clothes to my name. We were always short of money because of me always packing up my jobs.

After we had lived in the house for six years we were allowed to buy it from the council, leasehold, at a cost of three thousand eight hundred pounds £3,800 or freehold for four thousand three hundred pounds, £4,300, so we bought it on a mortgage freehold. I asked the man in charge of the houses at that time if I could buy the piece of land at the side of the house so I could build a garage. "If you promise to build a little wall and put up a six foot fence all around that plot of land

I will give it to you free of charge, and I will add it to your plans and deeds after twelve years," he said.

I did everything that was asked of me, and the man was delighted with the finished product, and so were we. Irene dug holes for that fence (it's still there to this very day thirty five years later). That piece of ground was eighteen feet wide and thirty six feet long. I dug out the foundations for my new garage and made it twenty three feet long and eight feet wide, with an up and over door at the front and a normal door leading to the back garden. I had it plastered, and put skirting boards in, and it was more like a study than a garage. It was a dream come true for me; it was my domain, my sanctuary, my shed, my playhouse. It's what all little boys dream of – it was my Den.

My job at that time was doing loft conversions all over the country. I drove a small Mercedes lorry; I used it like it was my car – I took it home and parked it on my drive all the time, and I never used my car at all, it was parked up in the garage. I even took Irene shopping in it, and we went for drives in the countryside on a Sunday. I sold my car and bought a Cedar conservatory from a firm called Kenkast and built it on the back of my house, we loved it. We built a wall all around the front garden out of those concrete bricks that were all the rage in the sixties and seventies. It was fifty feet long and three feet high. I had them delivered, and while I was at work, to my surprise when I got home from work Irene had carried every brick from the pavement to the back garden – that really pleased me, she is such a grafter is our Irene. The one thing that does make me smile, when we decorated the hall stairs and landing, which in my humble opinion is the worst place in the house to decorate, we were so pleased with it we sat on the top step of the stairs for what must have been an hour, may have even been more, that's youth for you.

As time passed, we found it hard to pay our mortgage, so after a very long discussion over many weeks in fact, we decided to sell our beautiful home. We went riding around the countryside; it was snowing and very cold, but we were on a mission so no snow or cold weather was going to stop us from finding our dream home. I had big ideas, trouble was I only had ten thousand pounds, which at the time

I thought was a fortune. We came across two cottages in Orton Road, Little Warton near Twycross Zoo in Warwickshire; they were numbered 102 and 104. They were two up and two down, no inside toilets, they were in a block outside, just like the one we had in Handsworth. They were the last two cottages in the village, and the views we thought were stunning. They where owned by an elderly couple who lived a couple of doors away. As we were looking, the old fella who owned them saw us and he asked if we would like to look over them. Of course we said yes. They were well run down! It was the old tin bath job in those cottages. Out the back belonging to the cottages was a large piece of land for growing vegetables, it was known as the man's garden and would you believe it women weren't allowed down anywhere near those gardens. The ladies had to shout to their men folk when it was dinner or tea time or one of the children would be sent to tell them. That was a shock to me, I can tell you. I was told this by a gentleman who was born in one of those cottages, his family were fourteen strong and next door were sixteen. Those poor women!

So after looking round, being young and foolish we both fell in love with them, and agreed we would buy them off him at a very large sum of seven thousand pounds. We shook his hand, and he agreed they were ours. We went into Atherstone to the agent and told him we were buying them, and the next day we went to our solicitors and started the ball rolling, as the saying goes. When all was signed sealed, we moved in. We got fourteen thousand five hundred pounds for Berwick's Lane house, that was May 1979, and we had two thousand pounds left after all the expenses were taken out. We had no idea what we had taken on – we bought with our hearts instead of our brains.

Irene and I were good labourers but our building skills were limited. We were given a grant from the council of three thousand pounds, and I pulled down the ceilings in the one house and lived in the other. On the landing I knocked through to the next cottage and did an arch, it looked great. I fitted a bathroom, got a plumber to fit central heating, that was solid fuel heating, dug up the floors and re-laid them with six inches of concrete – that was the regulations at that time. My eldest brother helped me to trowel up the floors, my younger brother helped me with bricklaying and rendering the house outside, and a carpenter showed me how to make ledger and brace doors – I even made a stable door leading from the dining room to the kitchen. I bought all the wrought iron door fittings for every door in the house. I fitted a kitchen, and I landscaped the front and back gardens.

I found a timber yard that sold reclaimed timber. They had twelve pitch pine lengths of timber fourteen feet long; I purchased them; they had come out of an old Chapel. How old they were I've no idea. They were eight inches deep, and six inches wide. It took me two weeks to strip all the old paint off them, and then I stained them with Jacobean stain, then I yacht varnished them – they looked beautiful. When I cut them to length one could smell the pitch pine, it's such a wonderful perfume, I kept picking it up and smelling it. With all the bricks I had knocked down inside the house I built an eight foot wall at the bottom of the garden. I made arches, four in all, that looked just like church windows. I also made an inglenook fire place in the living room with Ibstock smiling bricks, with a foot square oak beam, again in Jacobean stain and varnished.

I made the back door opening bigger and fitted a French window. I had to fit two seven by four RS Js, eight feet long, over the French windows first of course. I fitted those at night in the dark with the wind blowing, I had a sixty watt light bulb hanging on the wall and it was swinging in the wind. As I had two front doors, I bricked them up and put a new front door in the middle of the house, yes, that's what I had, a really big three bedroomed house. I had even converted the loft and put in a window in the gable end. During all this work I had a terrible chest infection and I was giving up smoking but because it was wintertime the work had to be done otherwise we would have all frozen to death.

In between all this I opened a shop in Stechford, plus running Irene to work and it took its toll on our marriage. People that lived in the village, whom I had never met, came knocking on my door asking if they could look round my house. It wasn't long before we were the talk of the village. We heard them saying what a wonderful job Irene and I had done, and I felt quite proud. I really enjoyed doing up those

My wife and I bought these two cottages. They were two up and two down. A gentleman who was born at number 104 told me that in one house there were 14 children, with parents that made 16. In the other cottage there were 18 people – at one time 34 people lived in these two cottages.

They were in an area know as Warton and were situated in a road called Orton Road. At the time of purchase they were 102 and 104. We made one dwelling out of the two. It then became 102. It was surrounded by countryside and oh so peaceful.

cottages, but it drove me away from Irene; it was a cottage too far I think.

The shop was my idea; Irene knew it wouldn't work but I would not listen to her. I opened it up as a hobby shop, selling fur fabric, matchstick kits and fur animals, but it didn't work. My nephew came to see me, he had been made redundant from the Co-op as manager of the delicatessen section, and he said if I change my shop into a cooked meats shop he would teach me the trade. He taught me well.

Then the recession hit, and I went broke and had to sell our cottages to pay off the debts. We had just enough money left to buy a council house. We sold the cottages for twenty one thousand five hundred pounds, and we left in July 1982.

We moved to Tile Cross in Birmingham, where we paid nineteen thousand pounds for a council house. We redecorated that house top to bottom. We sold it in May 1983, and moved to Whitebeam Road, Chelmsley Wood.

Irene found out she was pregnant, and that was a shock to both of us. She gave life to our third child, Matthew, on the 28th October 1983, two days before my fortieth birthday. Irene spent 44 hours in Marston Green Maternity Hospital. While she was in hospital I decorated some of the rooms for her to come home to with our new son. We paid £17,750.00 for that house, in May 1983. I made a pond and a waterfall in the back garden and I built a little wall with a lion's mask in the middle of it spurting water from its mouth. I laid down a plastic sheet from the bottom of the wall and into the pond. I went into the countryside around the Coleshill area, where the river Blythe flowed through, and paddled in that river and found big rocks. I did that trip three times, and back home I mixed up the concrete and threw it on the plastic sheet and after a while when the concrete was going off, looking at the rocks, I thought: when rocks fall and tumble down hillsides and mountainsides, they stop wherever, so I got the rocks, held them above my head and threw them in quick succession. They rolled and fell just as they would have in natural surroundings – the result was amazing. I placed plants in between the crevasses with a little soil and I placed some plants in pots – it looked so natural, all my friends loved it, in fact a couple of them tried to copy it but they tried placing the rocks in their ponds instead of just throwing them. I was just lucky; I made no fuss of it like I did with all the other waterfalls. We sold that house in March 1985, for twenty one thousand five hundred pounds £ 21,500.

We bought a semi-detached house in Castle Bromwich, number 65, Hawthorne Road, for £23,500. It needed lots of tender loving care, as the saying goes, so I thought I would be clever and start working on the house before contracts were signed. I went back to the agent who was selling the house to me and asked, "May I take another look around the house and take some measurements?"

"Yes, seeing as it is empty you can let yourself in, is that all right? And then when you have finished if we are closed just pop the keys through our letterbox," he told me.

"No problem," I replied. That's just what I was hoping he would say. I took the back door key off the ring and left the back gate unlocked, I knew the agent wouldn't notice, I popped the rest of the keys back through the letterbox as I had been asked. The next day I went back to the house and ripped out the bathroom suite, I took up the carpets, and over the next two weeks I fitted in a new bathroom suite, new carpets, cleaned up, and did lots of work in that house, and all before contracts were signed. On the day we were leaving Whitebeam Road, the lady that was buying our house came to pay me for a carpet we left. She said, "That was a scary moment this morning, wasn't it?"

I knew nothing. "What was?" I asked her.

She said, "The first-time buyers in the chain said they had changed their minds and weren't going to move." Her solicitor went to see the couple and explained if they didn't move they would have to pay all the expenses to everyone in the chain. This, I was told, frightened them, so they said they would move. I thought, and all that work and money I've spent on that house in Hawthorne road, I won't do that again. Well we moved and all went well for us, it was an easy move that day. We sold that house in March 1987.

Our next house that we bought was 24, Bentley Road, Castle Bromwich, and it was a repossession house – shame, they were a nice couple, just like us at Warton they ran out of money, but unlike us they just stopped paying their mortgage. We hadn't a mortgage, but we sold up to get out of trouble, they didn't. It's hard to leave a house that you have worked hard on for years, and then lose it, one has to take a deep breath and get on with life.

This house had been extended, I loved it; we decorated it top to bottom and landscaped the garden at the back. While I was sorting out the garden there was a large hole that used to be a pond, with a couple of inches of water in the bottom of it – all around the edge of the hole at the bottom were more frogs than I had ever seen before, they were shoulder to shoulder and every female had a male on her back. My son Matthew was looking at them, I said, "Don't stand on the edge of the hole, sit then you won't fall in." I turned my back, heard a splash, turned around and Matthew was sitting in the hole. He wasn't upset at all. I said to him with a smile, "What are you doing in there?"

He replied, "I'm talking to the frogs." I love that boy of mine. I set to, put all the frogs in a bucket and took them to Kingshurst Water Park. I filled in that hole. At the back of the house was a patio laid in 2x2 slabs, eight feet wide about eighteen feet long, so I set to to lengthen and widen it by putting more 2x2 slabs down. In the meantime we bought Matthew a little three-wheeled bike. Well I tried to show him how to peddle that bike but he just couldn't get the hang of it, so I carried on laying the patio slabs. It took me a week to get to lay the last slab. I stood, and to my shocked surprise, just as I laid the last slab, Matthew got on his bike and peddled round and round that patio; he pedalled for ages! He rode that bike on that patio daily; I was so pleased; it was worth all the hard work, in fact I was so pleased I took a photo of him.

Sometime after that, I've no idea why, I decided I wanted a divorce. I gave Irene a hard time, and I upset her more than words can say. I regret that time in my life. We are still the best of friends and we still help each other when it's needed. All the houses, rooms, shop, going broke and losing everything we had, worked for and lost, and built up again, I suppose it took its toll on me, I just lost the plot at that time in my life. We were divorced in 1992.

I bought a house in the same road, number 31 Bentley Road, and my then ex-wife bought a house in Hurst lane, Shard End, in December 1994. We helped each other to move houses. She made curtains for me and cleaned my house, and I bought a pack of central heating, boiler and all that goes with it for her. I got and paid a plumber to put in the central heating system, and I prepared the house ready for the heating so it would be quicker and Irene and Matthew wouldn't have to live in a mess for long. I fitted the kitchen sink in for her and bought her a new Metro car for her birthday so she could run my son about in a car that was reliable, and she did lots and lots for me.

I started on my house, and I was missing Irene something awful but I never told her. I was in my house for three weeks when the solicitor phoned me and told me I didn't own the head lease, there were eight people that owned it and they lived in America, Australia, New Zealand, Canada and Spain. It wasn't worth anything to them so they all signed and gave it to me. It cost me my solicitor's fees plus ten pounds, and I still don't know what a head lease is all about. Any road up, I bought the freehold; it cost me £3,000. As I walked over the front room floor downstairs I noticed it looked a little suspect so I got my crowbar and tried to prise up a floor board – the whole floor caved in, it was rotten, even the joists were too. To my surprise there was seven inches of water all over the ground under the floor so I went into the back room and inspected under the floor boards – it had been concreted and the floor was new, I'm glad to say.

After looking through the deeds and maps I found that the house had been built over a stream. It had been piped up, but it must have broken because it wasn't working, so I dug two long trenches the length of the room, five feet deep and filled them with rubble. In the kitchen I noticed the concrete floor was sagging, so with my sledge hammer I hit it in the middle, and it too caved in with me standing on it! There was an eighteen inch void under that concrete, the stream had washed all the soil away over the years. So again I dug a trench and filled it in with rubble. Outside in the back garden I dug two trenches ten feet in length and six feet deep and filled those with rubble, the reason I did them in the garden was that in the winter the bottom half of the garden

My son Matthew riding his bike for the very first time as I laid the very last slab. It was worth all that hard work to see him riding his bike.

Matthew two years later on. A bigger bike and still riding around the patio. It gave me much pleasure to see him enjoying his young life.

flooded really bad because the gardens either side of me were higher, it was the path the stream was in. One very early morning I heard a very loud crack – the guttering at the back had fallen off, so I went into the loft, and the twelve by three purling had snapped in half. I had a hole in the roof so I got a carpenter friend to help me erect a dormer, and we were doing that at a quarter to seven on Christmas Eve. When the summer came I had no washing facilities at all, no bathroom or tanks, only one floor downstairs, the only water I had was a stand pipe in the foundation that once was my kitchen floor, so I bought a new dustbin filled it with water and that's where I washed myself, in the garden in my underpants. I did that night after night for more weeks than I care to remember. There was a brick built air raid shelter built against the house with a slab of concrete on top, eight inches thick and six feet square. My younger brother John helped me knock it down. The slab of concrete we barred it on rollers to the bottom of the garden. We built two layers of bricks in a square, jacked up the concrete and got it on to the brick wall. I built a shed on it, built two steps up to it, built a two tier wall all around it on the concrete at the side of the shed, and filled it with soil. I then put flowers all around the shed – it looked great, everyone loved it. While I was doing that I had the house rewired and central heating installed, I made a shower room with black and gold tiles, I replaced all the floors, converted the coalhouse into a laundry room and fitted in a toilet so I had a toilet upstairs and down. I did a loft conversion, and finished the garden, so a rebuild and complete redecoration that had taken three and a half years was finished.

New neighbours moved in next door to me with two children. The little boy on the first morning they lived there was throwing stones at my front door. I had a leaded light window in it, and he cracked the glass. I chased him to his house, I was furious, the woman came out and I demanded to see her husband, but he wouldn't come out to see me. They had no control over their kids, so I put my house up for sale.

I got back with my wife, and we bought a house together – that was in 1998. The house was a large detached house in Springfield

Road, Castle Bromwich, just round the corner from my house. We paid £124,000 for that house and, it had every modern fitting that one requires these days – his and hers fitted bedroom furniture, a luxurious fitted shower, bathroom, a converted loft, polished wood everywhere, that house wanted for nothing. It had better carpets than we had ever had, a long rear garden all laid out, shed and a greenhouse, block paved front drive, walled all round, even a utility come laundry room. We again redecorated top to bottom, just to put our mark on it really but Irene couldn't settle there, nor my son Matthew, in fact none of us could, so it went back on the market. We had only lived there for three weeks. It sold in the hour for £135,000, and we parted company once more. I bought a house thirty yards away, 10, Oaston Road, while Irene moved to Laburnum Avenue in Kingshurst, just across from Castle Bromwich.

In my new house I dug up the floors, fitted central heating and a burglar alarm, changed and ripped out the old fireplaces and fitted new fireplaces, decorated top to bottom, half brick built a conservatory, fitted a toilet in it, fitted a new kitchen and put new carpets down and parquet floor tiles down the hall and right through to the kitchen, sanded and used Ronseal floor sealer – it looked great. In the meantime I moved Irene from Laburnum Avenue to Hawthorn Road, Castle Bromwich in July 2003. I did a lot of work for her; all the back garden as it was very overgrown, I cut down trees, weeded and tided up, and I fitted a new sink and toilet in the bathroom, but after a while she found it hard to run, as there were still lots of jobs to do. She put it on the market, but had some silly offers, the house boom had ended and she just couldn't sell it, so to help her out I sold mine and bought it off her. That was in January 2005 and I'm still here. The work I have done so far is, I have ripped out the entire bathroom and the airing cupboard, boarded all the walls and got them plastered, and run a cable from the meter board in the garage to the bathroom for a shower. I have fitted a new bathroom suite with the shower over the bath, painted and tiled around the shower, knocked a wall down in the kitchen into the extension, ripped out all the plumbing and the toilet that was in there and stripped all tiles from walls. I've replastered, fitted a new kitchen and divided part of the garage to make a laundry room, put a toilet in, a sink and washing machine, had it plastered, and it's now painted and tiled.

All the downstairs rooms are finished. I re-laid the patio with Irene's help and I've landscaped the back garden but not yet finished. I've had a new roof fitted, and put a new roof on the side entrance and fitted roof tiles instead of glass. In the garden is a brick built shed, which I have put roof tiles on instead of felt. There is still a lot to do but I am riddled now with arthritis, plus I've lost the will to do it anymore, I've lost complete interest – where I go from here, I have no idea. What makes it worse is I don't like it here, mind you I want for nothing, and my life is easier now I'm retired. Tired is the word.

I must add, without the help and support, even though we are divorced, from Irene, I wouldn't have this house as complete as it is today – thank you, Irene.

A POEM FOR MY WIFE

13TH of March is when we met

At the Castle Cinema, a meeting I will never regret.

First real love I ever knew

It was real love for me that I knew

I stroked your hair, I kissed your lips

I walked you home, my heart was mixed

Mixed up it was, I knew not why

You were my first love

My mind did fly

I was scared excited too

My heart it went from me to you

It never died just faded a bit

You were strong and kept hold of it

You knew when all the years had passed

Our love was strong and would always last.

***

SIMPLE PLEASURES

A friend of mine passed his test and got his H.G.V. heavy goods vehicle licence class one. He drove all around Europe. After about a year, he asked me if I would like to see Rome, and a lot of Italy – would I go with him to keep him company for a couple of weeks. His load was fifty-two tons of skins, sheep and cowhides.

We got the ferry at Dover early in the morning, hit France, travelled through to Italy, almost to Sicily, and we arrived at a lovely little village.

The skins didn't smell too sweet, I can tell you. When they were being unloaded it was dinnertime and a beautiful sunny day. The four ladies that worked there were gorgeous looking – that's all the workforce there was, four ladies. After the trailer was unloaded it had to be washed out and a perfume sprayed. The reason for this was we were picking up fifty-two tons of pasta, and the bosses of the factory inspected the trailer before they would load it. The drivers had to make sure there wasn't any blood anywhere. We met up with a driver from the same firm delivering a load of skins to the same firm; he too had to collect a lorry load of pasta.

When back on the road we followed the other driver. His artic was faster than ours, it had just come out of the workshop after being repaired and painted. He'd also had a new grill and an engine overhaul – he was very proud of his wagon. Any road up, we lost him and we took the wrong turning. We went through a town during rush hour, five p.m, and we were going over flyovers that had weight restrictions on them – the Italians were hanging out of their car windows crossing their wrists to indicate we could be arrested. We passed a police car at the bottom of the flyover, but as luck would have it they turned and were looking the other way.

We eventually got to a massive lorry park in Belgium where we met up with the other driver; it was a hotel for drivers, and I had a shower, and then washed and dried all my clothes. I had a lovely chicken dinner and spent some time in the rest room, it was very cosy and relaxing,

In Italy
Getting a full load of pasta to take back to England

then we returned back to the wagon, that's where we slept – it had two bunks inside the cab.

I was woken up in the middle of the night with what felt like an earthquake. While we slept the air brakes had failed, and we had rolled backwards nearly two hundred yards! It's hard to believe, but we passed a few wagons and hit the lorry from the same firm, the one that had just come out of the work shop. I asked my mate why he didn't leave it in gear, to which he replied, "I wasn't taught to leave it in gear." I couldn't believe what he had told me; I told him everyone knows leaving the wagon in gear acts as a brake. We had been sleeping on the top of mountains; the thought of that now makes me shudder!

When the other driver saw the damage to his cab, he had a fit and asked Andrew the same question I did. "Why didn't you leave it in gear!" he screamed. Andrew told him the same as he told me, he wasn't taught that way. "You never do! Are you mad? Look at my cab. I've only just had this back a few days and because of your stupidity it's got to go back in the workshop!"

The next day we loaded up with pasta. Andrew said, "You see all those boxes of pasta on the bottom layer, they will all be completely flattened by the time we get back in England," and sure enough, with the vibration and the bumping of the trailer, it did completely ruin the whole of the bottom layer the length of the trailer.

A simple pleasure we enjoyed on some Friday evenings was we sat in the car with our children eating fish and chips opposite the chip shop on a car park in the Tile Cross area of Birmingham. On occasions we sat in a lane that backed on to the Elmdon Airport, eating our fish and chips and watching the planes landing and taking off. We did this for our children to see the planes; it was lovely to see the excitement in their little faces when a plane took off.

Some years later when we lived in the countryside, we found a lane that overlooked old fashioned looking farm buildings that were deep in a dell. We were high up on a hill – it was so picturesque looking over that farm with rolling countryside all around. We loved that view so much. We sat in our car many times over the years, enjoying those beautiful views; Mother Nature is truly a wonderful thing.

Another place we used to visit with our children was called Little Packington. It was an isolated spot, and the river Blythe ran through it. At the side of the ford was a packhorse bridge that we crossed into a lane to walk and enjoy Mother Nature in all her glory. When it was a beautiful sunny day with the river glistening in the sunshine it was a very tranquil and peaceful place to be. It was on occasions a very popular place for families, who often took picnics when they took their children to paddle and catch fish with their nets. We made our nets from my wife's old stockings attached to a cane that I got from the pet shop – the joy of seeing our children enjoying life whilst paddling and catching fish, seeing water voles and kingfishers plus many different types of butterflies and wild flowers. We took a jam jar with string tied around the top for a handle; they got so excited when they caught a fish and put it in the jam jar so they could see what they looked like. We always put the fish back in the river, we never took them home. We taught our children to be gentle and kind to animals and the wildlife.

My children are grown up now, but while I'm writing this I'm wishing they were small again so I could take them to that river and see them enjoying life. My wife and I sometimes went to that same spot on our own, and as I stopped to look over the bridge that went across the river, I could see in my mind's eye my little children. What a wonderful feeling I have – while I'm writing this down I can see my little ones in that river enjoying life to the full. I loved those times and memories.

CHRISTMAS MORNING

One pleasure I had when I was young, just like most youngsters, was eating. One evening talking to my wife about life and the hardships that we had at times, Christmas came up. We were talking about food, well she was actually, and she said it was a struggle to feed me normally, not just on Christmas day. So we sat down and analysed what I used to eat on a Christmas morning. I was shocked, even horrified. When she actually went through the list of food I ate on a Christmas day this is how it went: After getting up, I went and sat down at the table, sometimes in an easy chair, and started to eat nuts, my favourite ones at that time were hazelnuts, plus sweets and fruit. When Irene brought in my breakfast it consisted of two rashers of bacon, two eggs, mushrooms, two sausages, a piece of fried bread, beans, tomatoes, black pudding plus four pieces of bread and butter and many cups of tea. All plates washed up and put away (by my wife, always by my wife) I would play with my children and their toys, and I would be eating more nuts, apples and oranges plus I would be eating sweets as well. Irene would be in the kitchen preparing the dinner and baking while I was filling myself with food.

As the table was laid for dinner, my plate would be piled high with a turkey leg and slices off the breast, a slice of pork, sprouts, peas, roast potatoes and boiled potatoes, but not stuffing, I don't like that. After all that was eaten, out came the Christmas pudding and custard. I love my Christmas pudding, I always had a dishful, and I love custard, and then I had many cups of tea. Back to the easy chair to watch the television, I would start again to eat sweets and fruit and nuts. I would eat right through to teatime, when again Irene would lay the table with a Christmas cake and mince pies, and she always made jelly, blancmange, sliced peaches, pears, trifle, a jug of cream, pork pie, sandwiches of turkey and not forgetting the Christmas crackers – we loved pulling the crackers at teatime. The children left the table when they had finished eating, and if they left anything like fruit or jelly I would eat that as well as any fruit, jelly or blancmange left in the big bowls. I must add at this moment in time, that my wife Irene loved her family so much, she never stopped running around after us; the perfect mother and a wonderful wife, she wouldn't let me anywhere near her kitchen; fantastic woman.

Back to the easy chair again to watching the television eating fruit, sweets and nuts, and then at suppertime I had turkey sandwiches. I ate all day long – nonstop, right up to bedtime. How did I do it? I have no idea, but I did it for many years. I don't drink beer or spirits, I'm teetotal, but I do drink tea by the gallon, even to this day. I must add, as a sixty-seven year old now my portions are much smaller, but I've never lost my taste for those jellies, blancmanges and trifles – I still have a very sweet tooth (well if I had any teeth, that is). My intake is still quite large at times (ha, ha), so am I; fat is probably a better word.

My son Anthony and my daughter Wendy

My son Matthew fishing in the river at Little Packington in Warwickshire where his older brother and sister fished many years before

My son Matthew with my granddaughter Holly, fishing in the River Blythe at Packington

This is the street where my dad was born.
Number 16 Queen's Street, Blaina, Wales.
Unfortunately some of the houses have been demolished. Dad's house was one of them. It was the house to the right of the blue car.

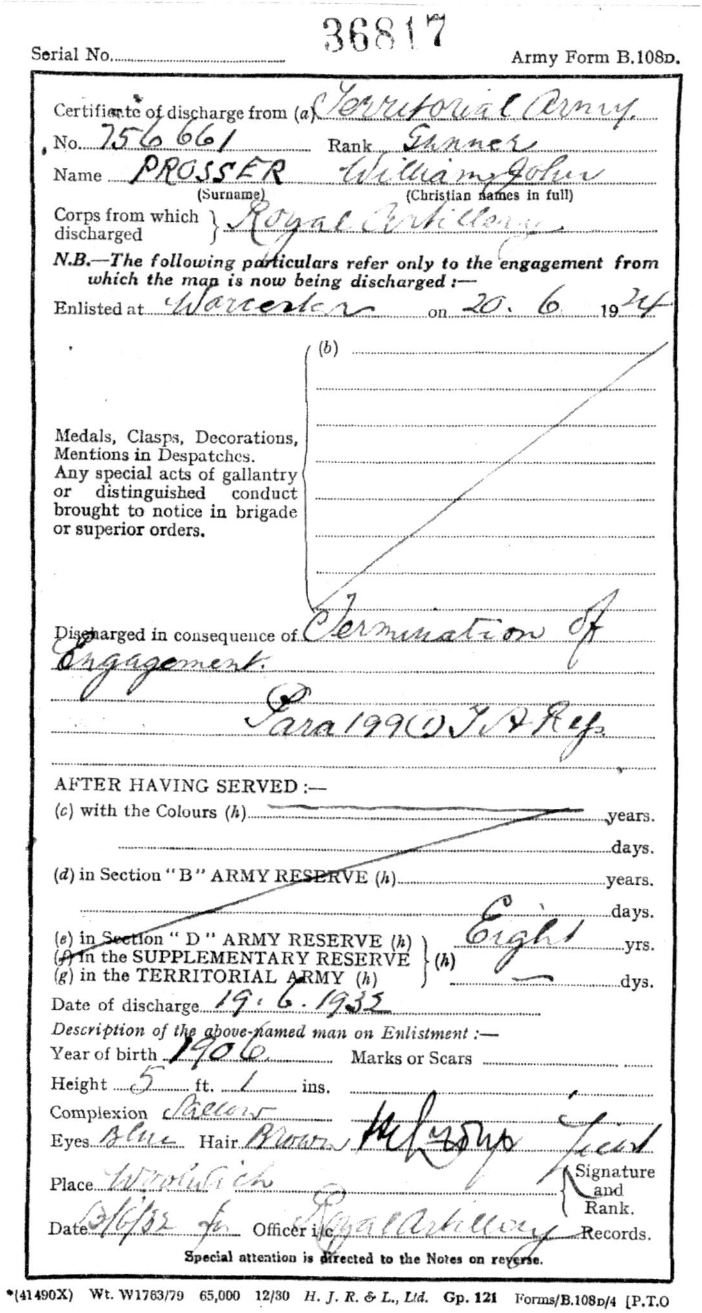

Serial No. 36817 Army Form B.108D.

Certificate of discharge from (a) Territorial Army.

No. 756661 Rank Gunner

Name PROSSER William John

(Surname) (Christian names in full)

Corps from which discharged } Royal Artillery

N.B.—The following particulars refer only to the engagement from which the man is now being discharged :—

Enlisted at Worcester on 20. 6 1924

Medals, Clasps, Decorations, Mentions in Despatches. Any special acts of gallantry or distinguished conduct brought to notice in brigade or superior orders. (b)

Discharged in consequence of Termination of Engagement.

Para 199 (i) T. A. Regs.

AFTER HAVING SERVED :—

(c) with the Colours (h) .... years. .... days.

(d) in Section "B" ARMY RESERVE (h) .... years. .... days.

(e) in Section "D" ARMY RESERVE (h)
(f) in the SUPPLEMENTARY RESERVE } (h) Eight yrs. — dys.
(g) in the TERRITORIAL ARMY (h)

Date of discharge 19. 6. 1932

Description of the above-named man on Enlistment :—

Year of birth 1906 Marks or Scars

Height 5 ft. 1 ins.

Complexion Sallow

Eyes Blue Hair Brown

Place Woolwich

Date 3/6/32 for Officer i/c Royal Artillery Records. Signature and Rank. Lieut

Special attention is directed to the Notes on reverse.

*(41490X) Wt. W1763/79 65,000 12/30 *H. J. R. & L., Ltd.* **Gp. 121** Forms/B.108D/4 [P.T.O

My dad's army papers 1924-1932.
Eight years training in readiness for the defence of England.

NOTES :—

(a) Here insert Section "B" Army Reserve, Section "D" Army Reserve, "Supplementary Reserve," "Territorial Army," as the case may be.

(b) The word "Nil" to be inserted where necessary.

(c) To be struck out if inapplicable.

(d) Applies to a Section "B" Army Reservist who fails to return to the O.i/c Records his A.F. B.108 for completion as to discharge. To be struck out if inapplicable.

(e) Applies only to men who enlisted direct into Section "D" Army Reserve and are discharged from that section and NOT to Section "D" Reservists who re-engage into that Section either from the Colours or from Section "B" Army Reserve. To be struck out in ink if inapplicable.

(f) Applies only to men who are being discharged from the Supplementary Reserve. To be struck out in ink if inapplicable.

(g) Applies only to men who are being discharged from the Territorial Army. To be struck out in ink if inapplicable.

(h) Each space is to be filled in and the word "Nil" inserted where necessary; numbers to be written in words.

(i) This Certificate is to be issued without any alterations in the manuscript.

WARNING.—The person to whom this Certificate is issued should on no account part with it or forward it by post when applying for a situation but should use a copy attested by a responsible person for the purpose. If the Certificate is lost it will be replaced only when its loss can be proved to have been due to very exceptional circumstances.

Application should be made to the Officer in charge Records.

Any alteration of the particulars given on the reverse of this certificate may render the holder liable to prosecution under the Seamen's and Soldiers' False Character Act, 1906.

DISCHARGE CERTIFICATE.

ANY PERSON finding this Certificate is requested to forward it in an unstamped envelope to the Under Secretary of State, The War Office, London, S.W. 1.

My Dad's Army papers 1924-1932 – eight years training in readiness for the defence of England.

Granddad King and Grandma King
and Aunty Margaret, bombed and killed in WWII

The three photographs on page 235, overleaf are of my mother's family. They all lived at number 53 Ash Road, Saltley, Birmingham 8.

Left is my granddad, Robert King. Right is my grandmother Clara King, bottom is my aunty Margaret King. In World War Two their house was bombed. My aunty Margaret was killed on the 10th April 1941. She was only 34 years old.

Her full name is Margaret Victoria Turland (nee King)
She is remembered on the Tree of Life Monument in the Bull Ring in Birmingham City Centre.

I also had an uncle Robert King, I haven't a photo of him.

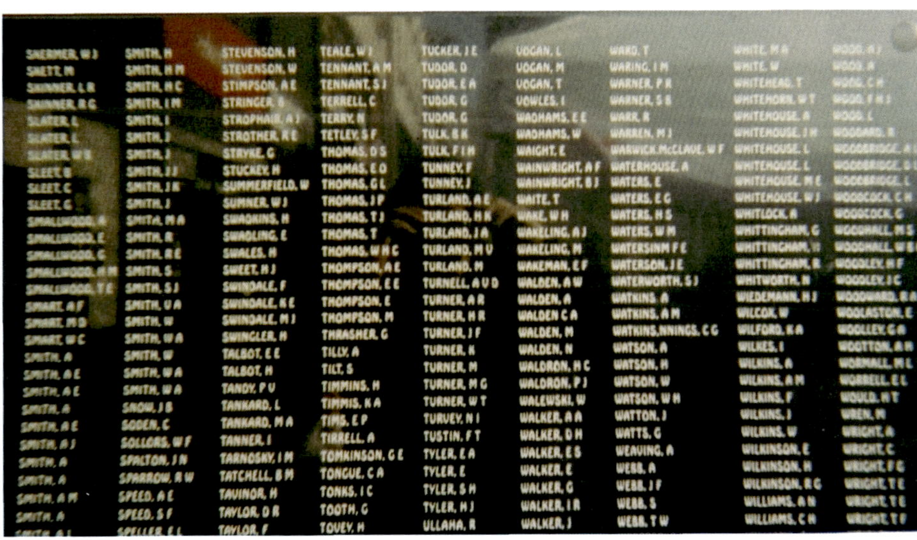

The monument showing my Aunty Margaret's name Turland, M.V

My parents' wedding in 1929
at
St. Saviours Church,
Ash Road,
Saltley
Birmingham 8

These are my brothers and sisters with our mom and dad.
Left to right:
Janet, Kenny, Donald, John, David, Doreen and Kathleen

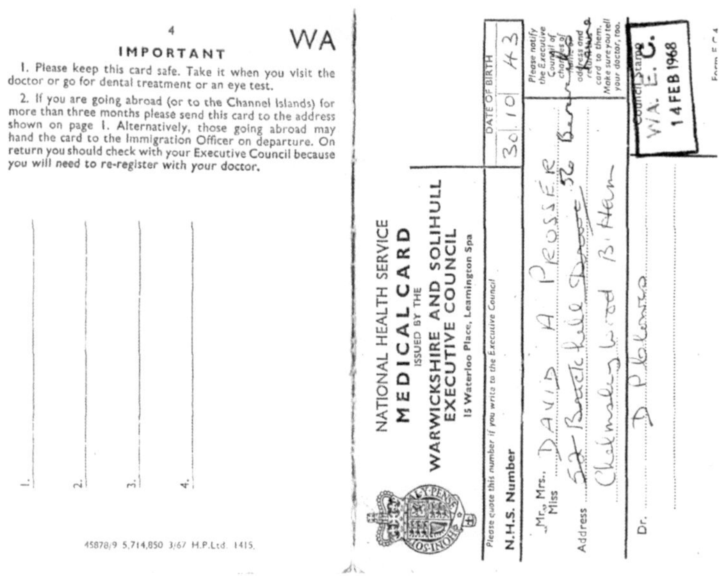
4

WA

IMPORTANT

1. Please keep this card safe. Take it when you visit the doctor or go for dental treatment or an eye test.

2. If you are going abroad (or to the Channel Islands) for more than three months please send this card to the address shown on page 1. Alternatively, those going abroad may hand the card to the Immigration Officer on departure. On return you should check with your Executive Council because you will need to re-register with your doctor.

1.

2.

3.

4.

45878/9 5,714,850 3/67 H.P.Ltd. 1415.

NATIONAL HEALTH SERVICE

MEDICAL CARD

ISSUED BY THE

WARWICKSHIRE AND SOLIHULL EXECUTIVE COUNCIL

15 Waterloo Place, Leamington Spa

Please quote this number if you write to the Executive Council

N.H.S. Number

DATE OF BIRTH 30 10 43

Mr., Mrs., Miss DAVID A PROSSER

Address

Dr.

Please notify the Executive Council of changes of name and address and return this card to them. Make sure you tell your doctor, too.

Council Stamp

W.A. E. C.

14 FEB 1968

My medical card issued on the 14th February, 1968

2

GENERAL INFORMATION

1. **Lists** of doctors, dentists and opticians taking part in the National Health Service can be seen at main Post Offices.
2. **Enquiries or complaints** about general medical, dental, ophthalmic or pharmaceutical services should be made to the Clerk of the Executive Council at the address shown on this card. A complaint should be made in writing and wherever possible within 6 weeks of the event which gave rise to it.
3. **Postage** must be paid on letters to Executive Councils.

YOUR N.H.S. DOCTOR

4. **This card** should be shown to your doctor if he asks to see it; if it is not produced he may charge a fee for which he will give an official receipt which contains instructions for the recovery of the fee.
5. **Day visits.** Please do not ask the doctor to call unless the patient is too ill to attend his surgery. Attendance at the surgery should be during surgery hours unless otherwise arranged by the doctor. When the condition of the patient does require a home visit, **please try to give notice, if at all possible, before 10 a.m. on the day on which the visit is required.**
6. **Night visits. Please do not call in the doctor between the hours of 8 p.m. and 9 a.m. unless you need him urgently.**
7. **In Accident or Emergency, first try to get your own doctor** (or his deputy). If he is not available, immediate treatment can be obtained from any doctor giving general medical services under the National Health Service.
8. **Temporary absence from home.** If you are away from your home district for three months or less, you can apply for treatment to any local doctor giving general medical services. Tell him you are a temporary resident *and quote your N.H.S. number.*
9. **Change of address.** If you change your address you may choose a new doctor by completing Part A on page 3. If you wish to continue to receive treatment from your present doctor, you should notify him of your new address immediately. You should also tell the Executive Council, at the same time sending this card.

3

10. ***Change of Doctor.*** *(a) If you choose a new National* Health Service doctor because you have changed to a new address, you and the new doctor should fill in Part A *below;* (*b*) If you wish to change your doctor for any other reason *either* (1) you may transfer at once with the consent of your present doctor and the new doctor; *Parts A and B below* should be completed by you and both doctors; *or* (2) you may write to the Executive Council (at the address on the front page of this card) saying that you intend to change. This card **must** be sent with the letter; it will be returned to you with the necessary instructions. You will not be able to transfer in this case until at least 14 days after the Council receive your letter.

Part A

*Drugs

Application to be placed on the list of

Dr...Date.........................

Signature of applicant ‡

....

†Rural Practice

Address of ....

applicant ....

Signature of accepting Doctor ....

Drs. Code No...Date.........................

Part B

Signature of consenting Doctor

I agree to this transfer.

~~Signature of accepting Doctor~~...

Drs. Code No...Date.........................

‡A person signing for the applicant should state relationship.
*If Doctor is to supply drugs he should enter D in space marked *.
†If Doctor claims a rural practice payment he should enter in the space marked † the distance from his main surgery to the patient's residence and should inform the Executive Council if he wishes to claim for units in addition to those for ordinary distance.

My medical card issued on the 14th February, 1968

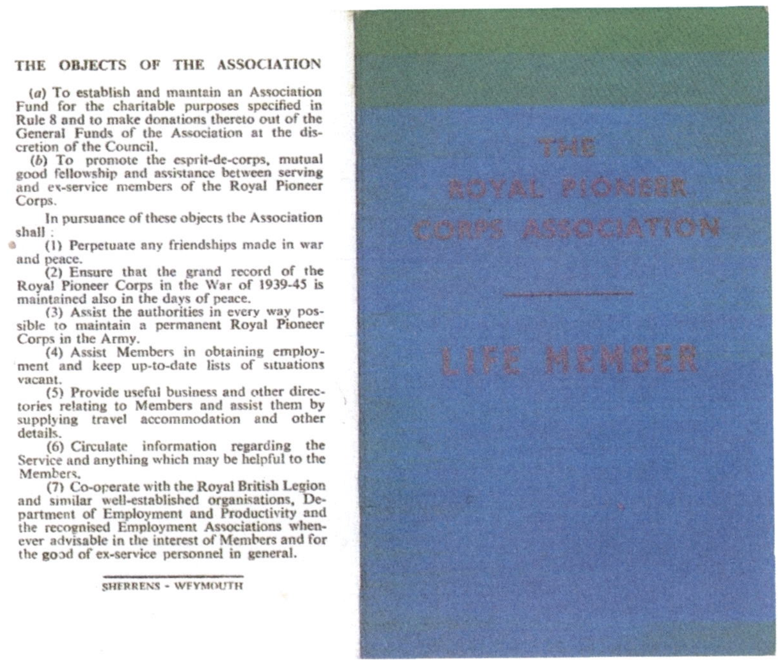

THE OBJECTS OF THE ASSOCIATION

(*a*) To establish and maintain an Association Fund for the charitable purposes specified in Rule 8 and to make donations thereto out of the General Funds of the Association at the discretion of the Council.

(*b*) To promote the esprit-de-corps, mutual good fellowship and assistance between serving and ex-service members of the Royal Pioneer Corps.

In pursuance of these objects the Association shall :

(1) Perpetuate any friendships made in war and peace.

(2) Ensure that the grand record of the Royal Pioneer Corps in the War of 1939-45 is maintained also in the days of peace.

(3) Assist the authorities in every way possible to maintain a permanent Royal Pioneer Corps in the Army.

(4) Assist Members in obtaining employment and keep up-to-date lists of situations vacant.

(5) Provide useful business and other directories relating to Members and assist them by supplying travel accommodation and other details.

(6) Circulate information regarding the Service and anything which may be helpful to the Members.

(7) Co-operate with the Royal British Legion and similar well-established organisations, Department of Employment and Productivity and the recognised Employment Associations whenever advisable in the interest of Members and for the good of ex-service personnel in general.

SHERRENS - WEYMOUTH

The Royal Pioneer Corps Association.
My life membership card.

The Royal Pioneer Corps Association

(Registered under
The Friendly Societies Act, 1896/48)

Registered Office :
51 ST. GEORGE'S DRIVE, LONDON,
SW1V 4DE
Tel. : 01-834 0415

President and Chairman :
General Sir NOEL THOMAS,
K.C.B., D.S.O., M.C.
(Colonel Commandant, Royal Pioneer Corps)

Patron : General Sir FRANK E. W. SIMPSON,
G.B.E., K.C.B., D.S.O.

MEMBERSHIP DETAILS

Regimental No. 24318077.

RANK Pte.

NAME PROSSER, D.A.

ADDRESS
56, Berwicks Lane,
Chelmsley Wood,
BIRMINGHAM, B37 7RE.

BRANCH H.Q.

Date of Joining 1/7/1975.

MEMBERSHIP No. L/4654.

General Secretary.

The Royal Pioneer Corps Association.
My life membership card.

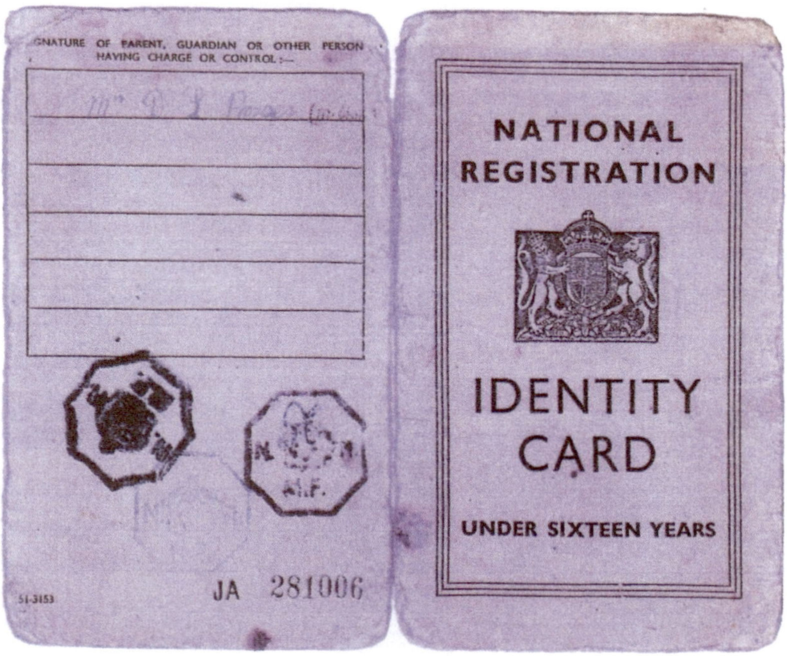

My National Registration Identity Card, 1943.

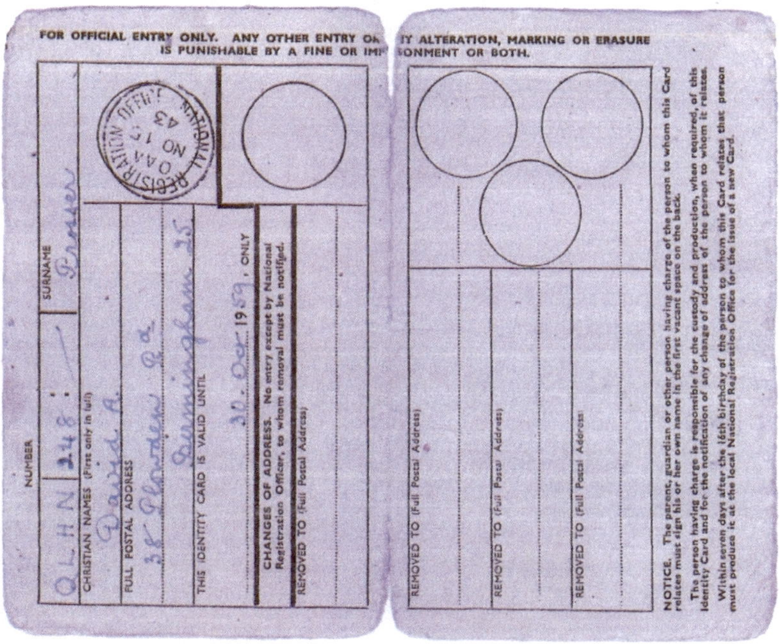

My National Registration Identity Card, 1943.

Author in the middle with his two sons
Anthony on the left and Matthew on the right

My family
Matthew's 18th birthday
Left to right, back row: Matthew, Mom Irene, Dad David
Front row: Anthony and Wendy

A POEM

Houses we bought houses we sold

We did this till we grew old

We dug trenches and knocked down walls

Ripped up carpets floorboards too

Papered walls so they looked new

Electric cables fitted too

Fitted bathrooms and showers new

To make our home look nice to view.

***

Other books written by

David A Prosser

Pumps With Holes In

Two Little Urchins

The Little Cottage Shop

Twenty-three Children's Stories

Just a Brummie

The Life of David A Prosser